MICHELLE J. FAYANT

LIFTED UP

*A Memoir of Overcoming Obstacles to
Find a Champion Within*

Misha Fayant

LIFTED UP

WI Publish

For information contact ; info@mishafayant.com
www.mishafayant.com

First Edition : May 2018

MISHA FAYANT

DEDICATION

This book is dedicated to the memory of my Pappa, Louis E. Fayant. He held me together when I was broken and taught me to keep getting up when I got knocked down. He will always be a motivating and stabilizing part of me.

LIFTED UP

MISHA FAYANT

CONTENTS

LIFTED UP

FOREWORD

An innocent little Native American girl born with so many struggles to face. Struggles that would scar her for the rest of her life, yet would also make her the free spirited, independent, strong woman she would become later.

She experienced the true meaning of racism, constant yelling, anger, and hate in her own home. The feeling of abandonment, physical, and mental abuse early on in childhood. Then as a woman, being controlled, the lies, infidelity, and yet again the feeling of abandonment, physical, and mental abuse ending in divorce.

Racism, unfortunately, is welcomed by people who are afraid. They will use labels, harsh and hurtful words, rather than investigate the unknown. Humans are afraid to learn what they do not already know. They will put up defense mechanisms and immediately assume and judge. They will run from the facts only believing the myths and the fiction.

She experienced the dark side and demons of the people she loved, those who she should feel safe with. Anger would rear its ugly head from those who were illustrated in books, in movies, and the families she had witnessed other than her own as being the true meaning of family.

Her Pappa was a man who she loved with all her heart and instilled in her the true meaning of what a real man should be, a man she trusted with all her being. Later in life she learned that not all men were like her Pappa. Pappa was a nurturer, a happy man, a jokester, a man of knowledge, and a man who sacrificed everything for his children until his last breath.

The love and respect for her Pappa motivated her to become more in touch with her Native American roots. This is one of the very few things that brought peace to her heart—keeping her in touch where she came from and who she was.

After guidance and unconditional love from those who were truly family, perhaps not by blood, but those of love and trust. She began

LIFTED UP

to believe in herself and trust those that loved her unconditionally and without stipulation.

Michelle began to create a vision in her mind that would trickle into her heart. Her dreams would then become reality. She allowed validation in herself and realized what a powerful woman she could become. She now has courage, strength, confidence, and doesn't feel the need of acceptance from anyone other than herself.

She is no longer that small, frail Native American papoose who felt so unloved and unwanted, but a strong female warrior who will always have the scars to remind her of where she came from, but never where she is headed.

She is a strong woman who feels deeply, and when she does love, she loves fiercely. She is a powerful, spiritual, and wise woman. She no longer speaks silently with inner mystery, but with inner beauty, confidence and strength. She walks with purpose, and she is now a woman with a voice.

I love you, Girlfriend.

Tam xoxoxoxo

INTRODUCTION

This book is by no means a complete memoir. It is simply a documentary of challenges that I faced that shaped my life, my mind, and as a result, my body. The challenges contained are meant to allow others to find that space of knowing that they are not alone and someone else has endured similar pain. These pages are meant to inspire, to provoke thought, to help someone—even one soul—heal from the scars of trauma, abuse, neglect, and abandonment.

There were many positive days in my life. This book, however, is about the dark things, the things that we all carry inside. The things that we stuff down until they force their way out in some form or another, whether it be physical symptoms or mental illness.

The story that follows was prompted after many clients, patients, friends, and peers encouraged me to share my story so that it may help others.

Everyone has trauma in their life and has experienced moments of rejection, neglect, or feeling not enough.   I share these pages to connect with others and show you are not alone. My hope through this book is to give hope to others that they, too, can become a phoenix rising out of their own ashes, whatever those ashes may be.

We are all human, we all have flaws, and we all have made mistakes. I believe the important part is, what you do with those "lessons"? Do you grow, or do you become a victim? WE all have a purpose no matter the circumstances in our lives.   We all have choices to make. Sometimes those circumstances and choices are not what you view as ideal, but what you make of them becomes your true story.

LIFTED UP

I hope that as you walk this path with me reading the pieces of my life that you find a way to find more love and acceptance for yourself through the pain, disappointment, and sorrow. They can be nourishment for your soul if you choose to use them this way.

CHAPTER 1

IN THE BEGINNING

*"Memories of childhood were the dreams
that stayed with you after you woke."*
Julian Barnes

Laughter and giggles rang through the house accompanied by the sound of tiny feet pattering on a wooden floor. Two young children scampered through the house playing and chasing each other through the stark prairie home, while a third child watched from his perch on the sofa.

Giggles turned into screeches and the children all ran and piled onto a bed where their father sat, a thin dark-haired man with skin the color of prairie clay, and eyes that shone blue as the summer sky. They all huddled around him. He was propped up at the head of the bed holding an old weathered shotgun. Once all the kids were safely on the bed, he gave one quick look at them, his blue eyes glistening as he smiled wryly. Suddenly he clicked open the barrel of the shotgun and shut it again with a quick snap; BOOM! He shot! The kids screamed and laughed, all safely piled on the bed around him.

That vision came through repeatedly in my childhood dreams. It appeared as a dream but felt like a memory, one of those knowing warm sensations that felt as if from a movie or story told.

LIFTED UP

Apparently, we did live in a little home out on the Montana prairie when I was a toddler. At the time, Dad was so ill he could barely get out of bed. The doctors had no idea what was wrong with him and were really just waiting for him to die. During that time, us kids were often left home with him while Mom went to work to support us. According to him, we had rats, and he would gather us all on the bed when they would appear and shoot at them to try and kill them off. The "dream" was a memory— one of many that came flooding into my consciousness later in life.

In that same house a short, stout, leather skinned man sat on a square looking couch. A little girl was in the kitchen where a clanking could be heard of metal on glass. The mother yelled, "Get out of there!" The little girl rushed, tiny legs peddling as fast as they could to the safety of that leather skinned man. Her grandpa, my grandpa, was waiting for me with open arms on that couch. He snatched me up and gently, firmly sat me on his knee, and hugged me tightly. I looked up into his bright eyes to see a grin spreading across his face, like the Cheshire Cat from Alice in Wonderland. Mother came from the kitchen still yelling at me. Grandpa held me even more tightly and looked defiantly at her saying, "You leave my girl alone, or you will deal with me". Mother huffed and glared at him, her eyes momentarily furious then turned and headed back to that kitchen tucked away behind a wall.

My little native grandpa would then sit for hours, bouncing me on his knee. He sang songs to me, some in French that I did not understand, but laughed at anyway and some in English (very few). But the song I remembered him singing the most was, *"Michelle, my belle, those are words that go together well, my Michelle."* I felt so special, loved, and protected when Grandpa was around, but he lived far, far away, and we did not get to see him very often.

Wintertime in North Idaho can be unforgiving. The cold can chill you to your bones. Our little family had just moved from the mountain prairies of Montana to the forest mountains of Northern Idaho. My parents found a piece of remote property to the north of a little town in the mountains near Canada.

I remember the first time driving up that bumpy old dirt road into the thick evergreen forest. Excitement was in the air, and my brothers and I could barely sit still! Mom was trying to keep us contained. Dad was antagonizing us kids as usual: teasing, driving erratically, and singing songs. It felt like an eternity before we pulled up to a small clearing. In that woodland meadow stood an old weathered barn-like building, sun beating down on it, bringing some joy through the trees to illuminate the tattered old structure. This was going to be our new home!

A small, singlewide trailer was soon placed on that property. It was tiny—only about 8 feet by 36 feet. The front end had a couch built-in that spanned the width of the home. The kitchen stood just past it, and a small table pushed against one sidewall. Just behind the kitchen was the bedroom where my brothers and I slept. Really, it was a double bed on the bottom and a twin bed on top, tucked into the wall. The hallway going right through the middle of the home had dressers below and a closet built over into the opposite wall.

Behind that was the bathroom, then through that small bathroom at the very back of the home was my parents' bedroom. There were two entrance doors to that tiny house, one at the front by the living area and one at the back in my parents' room. The toilet inside was not functional, as it had no sewer yet, so we had an old-fashioned outhouse in the yard that we used for our bathroom.

As kids, we did not mind the tiny house. I can only imagine my mother's frustration trying to run a household in that miniscule space with 3 rambunctious kids bouncing off the walls and constantly under her feet. I honestly don't know how she did it. We were smack in the middle of nowhere. To us kids, it felt like an adventure. I have many memories from that home even though I was very young.

LIFTED UP

We had a mischievous black cat. One Sunday, we all packed up and headed to church. Mom had left a roast thawing on the counter. When we arrived home, Mom entered the house to find that roast destroyed by the cat. She was horrified! Dinner was gone. We did not have much in those days, and we were far from any grocery store or civilization, so it was a significant loss.

Dad entered the house to find Mom angry, red faced, and pushed to her boiling point. She was panicked over what had happened. Dinner was gone! He grabbed a broom and started chasing that black cat through the house, kicking at it, swatting at it with a broom and yelling at it, "You black son of a bitch!" He shouted over and over.

I followed him, kicking at that cat and yelled "black sombitch" with my most serious and angry little girl voice. Oh boy! That was not the way a young girl talked! I was grabbed by the back of my neck by Mom and hauled to that tiny bed in the back. I was then spanked soundly and told to stay there because I had sworn, and I had a filthy mouth.

As a young girl, I did not understand. I was just doing what Dad was and following his lead. As an adult, I can laugh and see the frustration and complete absurdity of that moment and time. Dad remembered that day as well, and we often joked about it as I grew into a woman. Occasionally, he would look over at me with that oh too familiar gleam in his eyes, and he would exclaim, "Black sombitch!" then burst out in full belly laughter, cracking up about the memory.

That house in the northern woods was also a playful, wonderous place. Dad was as mischievous as they come, always finding some way to cause havoc and create his version of fun. He was my superhero. He was fearless. He was funny. He was strong, determined, and unstoppable in my mind.

Winter came, and we had plentiful snowfall. The snow was deep and wet, and us kids just wanted to get out and play in it! We wanted to go sledding, but the hills around us were all covered with pine, tamarack, cedar, and other evergreens so dense there were no places to sled but on the backwoods' winding dirt road. Most importantly, we did not have sleds!

The hills were too far from the house for Mom to let us trek out on our own, so of course, Dad devised a plan. He took the hood from an old car, fastened ropes to it, and tied it to the back of his truck. We were going to go sledding!

His eyes sparkled. He was such a fun soul. He demanded we all bundle up and get to the pickup. We all packed into that little pickup and started down the road. When we arrived at the hilly spots, he told us to get out and get on that old, cold car hood and hang on tight.

We were so excited! Adventure! Snow! Snow still falling, the three of us kids clamored out of the truck and took our positions on that piece of metal lying in the deep snow.

Dad shouted, "Ready?" Then he took off building speed to get up the hill. It was so much fun! We did not even notice the cold. The roads wound through the trees, and up, then down carving their way through the North Idaho mountains.

We bumped and tossed around holding on for dear life, squealing and cheering in the brisk winter air. The snow fell around us in a soft mist of cool white, making the day feel mystical and magical.

Dad found a place to stop and turn around, so we got off and waited impatiently to ride again! Going down was so much faster than going up! It felt like we were on a snow rocket. Up and down the humps in the road and around curves we went, faster and faster. One curve, the truck began sliding in the deep wet snow. The "sled" went flinging back and forth behind it, finally tossing us off over the hill and into the woods.

LIFTED UP

Mom screamed! She would get so frustrated with Dad. Who could blame her? He was the coyote incarnate (a Native American trickster). As soon as the truck stopped, she went running to find us and make sure we were okay. To her relief, we all three survived, but that would be the end of that days' adventure.

CHAPTER 2

THE RUGARU

"In the dark of the night they will come for the bad children,
the children who disobey, so be good
or the Rugaru will get you, too."
Louis Fayant

That little home held so many memories for me. Being Native American, Dad told stories from his childhood of the Rugaru. The Rugaru consisted of many varying stories based on the same theme, a demon that took the shape of an oversized black animal that sought to hunt down people who misbehaved or did immoral things. The Rugaru would come out in the night in search of it's prey.

From an online source at Wikia:

"It is important to note that rugaru is not a native Ojibwa word, nor is it derived from the languages of neighboring Native American peoples. However, it has a striking similarity to the French word for werewolf, loup garou. It's possible the Turtle Mountain Ojibwa or Chippewa in North Dakota picked up the French name for "hairy human-like being" from the influence of French Canadian trappers and missionaries with whom they had extensive dealings. Somehow that term also had been referenced to their neighbors' stories of Bigfoot. Author Peter Matthiessen argues that the rugaru is a

LIFTED UP

separate legend from that of the cannibal-like giant wendigo. While the wendigo is feared, he notes that the rugaru is seen as sacred and in tune with Mother Earth, somewhat like bigfoot legends are today."

One story Dad told us:

One of his uncles was constantly going out drinking and carousing with random women, single and married alike. His mother warned him not to continue these behaviors and evil ways or the rugaru would surely come for him. He had just gotten into some trouble with law enforcement for going out and getting drunk, causing problems in town, and being disorderly in public. He was ordered to stay home and not go out for a period of time. Not soon enough, his time had passed, and he was restless, ready to drink, and wanting to socialize.

It was wintertime, and he had taken all he could of being locked up in the house. Temperatures were low, and the ground covered in snow. Still, he decided he was going to go out. He was going to get out and do something no matter what! He waited until everyone was busy or asleep and quietly snuck out of the house, heading down to the local pub. He stayed out all night drinking and carousing with the women who were out until he could barely stand. When the pub closed, he had to face the long walk home.

On the way home, he heard heavy footsteps that did not seem normal behind him. He was too drunk to function properly, but he decided to speed up his slow pace. As he sped up, so did the footsteps. He stopped. The footsteps stopped. He was beginning to sober up a bit in the bitter, cold snowy night. He turned to confront whoever may be following him, thinking he may have offended someone at the pub.

To his horror when he turned, he saw a large black wolf/dog, eyes burning red, and fire blowing from his nostrils. It was dark, and the wolf was in the distance, snarling and glaring at the young man. He turned and began to run for his life toward the house. He could hear the footsteps speeding up, growing closer; he was terrified he would be eaten and never to be found again. Just as the creature closed in on him, he arrived home and bounded through the front door, slamming it behind him. He leaned his body against the door to hold it shut for fear the creature would come through. Just then, his mother came into the dark room carrying a candle. She was about to reprimand him when she saw his face and heard his trembling breath, still leaning against the door.

"What is it!" she exclaimed. "What happened?"

He looked at her and shouted, "The Rugaru! He is after me!"

She smiled wryly and began berating him, "I told you not to go out. I told you your evil ways would draw his attention. Do you believe me now? Are you going to straighten up now?"

Still trembling, he slumped to the floor and vowed never to go out and be drunk and pay attention to the wrong women. He vowed to behave and stay home and live a clean life.

There were many stories. Sometimes it was the wolf. Other times, it was a huge black horse. Always it was the same thing: burning red eyes and flames flaring from his nostrils.

There was also the story of a large, screeching bird who hovered over the villages, searching for misbehaving children to feed on. This one was more horrifying because it happened even in the light of day!

One day, a young boy was sent out by his mother to go fetch a pail of water at the water pump. He had been naughty all day. He spent his day disobeying her at every turn. The mother was at her wits end with him. Frustrated and needing water to cook and clean dishes, she sent him out the door with the pail in hand.

It was a bright, sunny day, and he wanted to play. As soon as he stepped out the door, he forgot what he was sent to do. He dropped

LIFTED UP

the pail and ran off to find something to entertain himself. Soon his mother began calling for him. She needed that water!

He did not respond. He was too busy playing in the prairie grasses. From inside the house, the mother could hear the loud flapping of giant wings. The sound was deafening, and it shook the little house.

Realizing what it was, the mother screamed! The bird rugaru had come to take the boy for misbehaving. She ran for the door, but she was too late. When she flung the door open bursting into the bright sun, all she could see was the boy dangling from the bird's talons. That enormous bird carried him away. As it soared, flying into the sun, it screeched a deafening, piercing warning to notify everyone of his success in catching his prey.

The little boy was gone never to be found again. We were warned to behave and to do as we were told and to be good little kids. No fighting, no disobeying mother or father, or else!

As kids, we could only imagine the horror of this massive creature coming for us in the night if we misbehaved. Remember, to make matters worse, we used an outhouse!

The stories were an attempt to keep us kids in line, but they terrified us! I hated going out to the outhouse in the night. I was sure that I had done something wrong during the day that would cause the rugaru to find me in the dark and eat me before I could get back to the house.

There were many nights when I woke, as I felt the sharp pressure of a full bladder needing release. Suddenly, terror filled my gut. Often on those nights I laid frozen in bed, too scared to get up and make the perilous trek to the outhouse. The outhouse that seemed miles away in those dark, foreboding northern woods. Those nights lying awake trying to hold my bladder, afraid to stay, but more terrified to get up,

I would inevitably feel the sudden hot steam as my little body could no longer hold it in.

I had been told what a horrible little girl I was so often that I accepted those terms on my life. I was certain that if I stepped out of that door into the cool black night I would most assuredly be eaten by the Rugaru who I just knew was standing guard waiting for me to make my final mistake. Mom would get so frustrated at the midnight disruptions, and Dad would just laugh.

Those rugaru stories kept me on the straight and narrow for many years. They also kept me afraid of the dark. Even into adulthood, I could not sleep with any part of me uncovered or hanging off the bed. Irrational as it was, I had this inner fear the demon would come drag me from my bed and make me his dinner if any part of me was exposed or hanging off the bed.

"Human beings, we have dark sides;
we have dark issues in our lives.
To progress anywhere in life,
you have to face your demons."
John Noble

LIFTED UP

CHAPTER 3

SCARRED AND BURNED

"Childhood trauma does not come in one single package."
Asa Don Brown

It was in that tiny house that I was first burned. Mom had been cooking, and my brothers and I were playing and running through the house. I got under her feet in the kitchen and a pot of scalding hot water dumped over my legs. The heat was searing. Immediately, my legs felt like I was standing in that pot of boiling water. I screamed! Mom screamed. I looked down and saw my skin bubbling, boiling up with blisters that covered my little legs from the knees down. I was put in a bath of cold water, but the blisters had already formed.

"I looked down and saw my skin bubbling."

The next morning was a school day. It was wintertime in Northern Idaho in 1970. It was cold, so we needed to bundle up. Wool socks were the wintertime staple for cold feet and legs back then. Mom

23

placed the socks on my feet and legs, right over the blisters and sent me off to school. Youth can be an amazing thing. Young minds can be so oblivious to so much, so focused on play and the "important" immediate things in life that you don't notice the small things. I remember my legs hurt, and they felt wet off and on throughout the day, but I had things to do! I was with other kids, and I was in school. I loved learning.

In those days, there were two sets of clothes for us all. The clothes we wore to town, school, or church, and the clothes we wore for play and at home. Everyday coming home meant changing from our "good" clothes into our "play" clothes.

That day returning from school, I changed out of my school clothes. I got down to my socks, but they would not come off! They were stiff, hard, and stuck firmly to my legs. I had no idea what was wrong, so I went to tell Mom I could not get my socks off. She was angry at first that I was being so stupid that I could not take off my own socks. Then she touched them, those cardboard like things did not resemble socks anymore.

Panic set in. What were we to do?

She held me down and began pulling the socks from my legs. The blisters had all popped from the pressure and coarseness of the socks, and the socks had healed into the flesh on my legs. Taking them off meant ripping skin from my legs.

I screamed hysterically and begged her to stop. My stomach felt like acid inside from the pain. My body shook, I screeched, and wailed. She enlisted the help of my brothers to hold me down while she ripped the socks off my legs removing chunks of flesh as she pulled.

I will never forget feeling ill from the searing pain and the thought of my skin being ripped off my legs. I looked down and saw blood. My legs were raw, bleeding, and stinging in pain. My skin was still stuck to the socks that had been on my legs. I was horrified!

MISHA FAYANT

As a child I could not understand why she did that to me. My perspective as a child differed greatly from hers as an adult. As a child, seeing the intensity in her eyes and the anger she displayed as she ripped those socks from my legs terrified me. I wept inside: my head reeling, feeling hopeless, and helpless. To me, it was just another display of how much she disapproved of me, disliked me, and did not want me around.

It scarred me. It was the first of many times having some hot liquid poured over my head, coffee, stew, and more boiling water covered me multiple times. Each time, the physical and emotional scars from the burns, deepened, the wounds widened, and I became surer of how unwanted I was. Not just unwanted, but despised.

Combined with other factors, my little psyche began to hold to the fact that I was hated. It was the story I began to build in my own mind. These things did not happen to my brothers, only to me. My subconscious began to file those things away, making a case for how much I was unloved.

"Sometimes I think we're exposed to things we shouldn't be exposed to too early. I think that sets the tone to a person's whole life. Trauma."
Tracy Morgan

Having done extensive personal growth as an adult coupled with healing work, I can now look back and see the misfortune and detach it from the abuse that I once thought was there. I can now see a young mother—her hands full, three kids, a mischievous husband, and the demands on a woman during those times.

LIFTED UP

It turns out that the illness Pappa suffered while we were in that little house in Montana was due to silver dissolving into his blood stream. He had been run over by a car when he was small, crushing many bones in his little body including his toes. When he was a child, the doctors did not know better and used silver in pins and rods to attempt to repair his toes. That silver was apparently entering his blood stream as a young adult and poisoning him slowly. Being the stubborn, strong man, he was, he survived what would have killed most men.

His toes never recovered though! His feet looked like a mangled mound of worms where the toes should be. It was curious to me. As a child, I looked at those toes and wondered how he got that way and how he could walk with them like that.

After he recovered from blood poisoning, he returned to work full force. He was always a driven man—a workaholic. Dad's work meant that we had to travel at times. One of those times meant a temporary move to a small home in Southern Idaho.

In those days we had our mouths washed out with soap every time we lied or swore. Swearing was inevitable, because we had a Dad who consistently let loose, dropping gems in the form of forbidden words for us kids to pick up and use.

I ate enough soap as a small girl that I felt like I would poop bubbles. Some days, I would just go get the bar of soap without being prompted. It was worth it! Defiant, somedays, I just could not help it.

That house had a deep closet in my room that went back behind the wall. It was my first experiences as an introvert. I would go in that closet and shut the door. Sitting quietly in the dark gave me some comfort and peace. At least my two brothers were not pestering me constantly.

My older brother Louis was stout, dark haired, strong willed, and the oldest. So of course, he was domineering over my younger brother

Robert and me. My younger brother, who had been born prematurely, was skinny, wiry, and into things all the time! He reminded me of the old Speedy Gonzales cartoon, running here and there at the speed of light.

Sometimes it was too much for me, so off to my closet oasis I would go. More than once, I fell asleep in that closet unnoticed. That was fine by me.

We eventually moved back to Northern Idaho. This time Dad bought a 5-acre tract of land outside of town and began clearing the forested acres to make space for our new home.

Trucks and storage containers full of the pieces of our lives parked at the back of the acreage. They held our furniture, photos, clothes, tools, and all that was us until our home could be placed.

It was exciting running wild in those woods as a kid and playing hide and seek with my brothers and cousins in the trees. One of our favorite places was an old homestead cabin that had only the foundation and part of the walls. Maybe it was never finished, but we loved going to that spot deep in the woods and playing all sorts of war games and homestead games. With two brothers, it was most often war games! We were always hiding behind the rough-hewn logs pretending to be shot at, dodging the bullets in our minds, and running for safety from the invaders.

It felt like our own Adventureland in those woods, full of hiding places and wonder.

We made new friends there, and together we spent many hours walking the woods to get between our homes. Sometimes the trip meant walking down the gravel road that seemed miles long to a young body.

One family became our close friends. They had a girl a year older than me and a boy about the same age as my older brother. We spent many days and evenings at their home playing games.

LIFTED UP

One game that everyone loved to play was called "Spoons", a card game that was fast paced and rowdy. Each round had one less spoon than people playing. Inevitably, there would be a "fight to the death for that last spoon."

One night, one of my parents and the woman whose house we were at fought for the last spoon, both of them sprawling across the table tugging, back and forth, pulling and shouting. Tooth and nail, they fought for that spoon until the weight and the violence of their tumultuous fight broke that table right in two!

CHAPTER 4

GROWING UP HALF BREED

"This war did not spring up on our land, this war was brought upon us by the children of the Great Father who came to take our land without a price, and who, in our land, do a great many evil things... This war has come from robbery – from the stealing of our land."
Spotted Tail

Playing games and having a few drinks, my parents and our neighbors decided to continue late into the night. Darkness was looming, my two brothers and I were sent home on a quest to beat the dark night. Our trek was found walking that gravel road in the country. It was dusk. Worrying about being caught out in the dark, prey for the rugaru, my heart raced keeping my feet moving. The air was still and fresh, the pine trees stood stately guard on our path home, watching as we passed by, quietly observing as we kicked up gravel, laughing, and tormenting each other as we walked, and then sped down the road toward home. Safe! We made it before the darkness swallowed us up!

Playing and getting ready for bed with the pitch-black mysterious night surrounding us, the phone rang. We were still home alone. Answering the phone, the voice on the other end was a man's voice. It was deep and angry. The message that was about to be

LIFTED UP

delivered could not have been expected. Cursing, degradation, warnings and threats came raging through the phone line. As he spoke, his voice became increasingly agitated until he was yelling as he ended his message for me.

In very certain terms, I was informed of how my life was not worthy of being on this planet, how dirty and lowly I was, and how dogs and even cows had more worth than me. Seething he let me know I deserved to die. He and "friends" from town would come to kill us all. We would not know when. Native American, and worse for me, an abomination half-breed, our heritage, burden, and our death sentence—rage and vengeance toward me, my brothers, my family was delivered because of that bloodline. Racism was alive and well.

Calls kept coming, all similar. It left me with a chill, hair standing on the back of my neck and an ache deep in my gut. Huddled up, overwhelmed, and beginning to feel fear, I heard noises outside scratching like an animal trying to claw its way into our home, followed by a deep guttural growling. Moving around the house, scratching and scraping on the walls.

"The scars and stains of racism are still deeply embedded in the American society."
John Lewis

The three of us were so terrified; we dared not look out the window to see what was there. Was it a bear? Or worse yet, had the rugaru come at last to eat us up and end our little lives. The screams from inside the house eventually drowned out the growls and scratching from outside. We were all huddled in a ball, trying to hide from whatever it was out to get us. The scratching moved to under the house, and we were certain that whatever it was, would come right through the floor of the double wide mobile home we were living in to claim us as its bloody prey. Just when we could take no more, it stopped and disappeared as quickly as it came.

It was some time later before we learned that it was Dad playing a prank on us. He had no idea about the phone calls I had endured that night that heightened my state of terror.

After that night, every time I went to town I was constantly looking over my shoulder trying to figure out who it was that called—who was lying in wait to take my life when I least expected.

It was the early 1970's and there was unrest between the Native Americans and the US Government. AIM (American Indian Movement) was gaining ground among the Native peoples across the Nation, and it terrified white people. Us "heathens" were finding a voice and becoming active in pushing back against the terrors that had been consistently perpetrated against us for many years. The BIA (Bureau of Indian Affairs) was becoming more involved from the government side trying to neutralize the growing voice and movement of the average Native American.

The Billy Jack movies came out and mirrored the injustices and genocide of our peoples by the United States people and Government. We, as Natives, were forbidden to gather in groups of more than 5 or face punishment and be arrested. We could not gather to worship, commune, or mourn outside of these restrictions. In secret, we would head out to meetings in the dark of night— meetings that changed place each time we went, to hide the fact that we were gathering unlawfully.

Many of the meetings involved the playing of the Billy Jack movies. It was traumatizing as a young girl to watch the stories of rape and murder being played on the movie screen before our eyes. Stories our parents knew we had to see, stories that must be told. The film was a depiction of the reality of our daily lives as Native Americans.

LIFTED UP

Billy Jack is a "half-breed" American Navajo Indian, a Green Beret Vietnam War veteran, and a hapkido master.

Jack defends the hippie-themed Freedom School and students from townspeople who do not understand or like the counter-culture students. The school is organized by Jean Roberts (Delores Taylor).

A group of children of various races from the school go to town for ice cream and are refused service and then abused and humiliated by Bernard Posner and his gang. This prompts a violent outburst by Billy. Later, the director of the Freedom School, Jean, is raped and an Indian student is then murdered by Bernard (David Roya), the son of the county's corrupt political boss (Bert Freed). Billy confronts Bernard and sustains a gunshot wound before killing him with a hand strike to the throat, after Bernard was caught in bed with a 13-year-old girl. After a climactic shootout with the police, and pleading from Jean, Billy Jack surrenders to the authorities and is arrested. As he is driven away, a large crowd of supporters raise their fists as a show of defiance and support."
Wikipedia

To this day, the average person has no idea of the slaughter of innocent schools full of Native children in my lifetime, of the eugenics planned and played out by prominent politicians reaching as high as the Commander in Chief. Most people do not want to hear and do not want to know the things that have happened. Because of it, they will vehemently deny any recounting of the tragedies that occurred. Today, most people are in shock and utter disbelief when I retell the stories of my life. Keep in mind; my stories are nowhere near the things that happened to my relatives who lived on the reservations.

For a time, we had to wear armbands when we left our homes to signify that we were native. If caught outside of our home without these red bands on our arm, we were threatened with immediate detainment and jail. Even the youth were forced to comply.

It was a time of tremendous unrest: dead bodies showing up in the Kootenai river, reports of the CIA, BIA, and AIM representatives being camped out in hiding, watching the valley where we resided, and ready to act as needed.

There was a mixed feeling of pride and fear that went with leaving our home during those times. Putting on those red armbands as part of our attire was crucial. Everyone in town seemed to know who the natives were, and they were on the lookout for those of us not donning our required attire.

"Even a small mouse has anger. "
Tribe Unknown

The trip to town was only a 5-mile trek, and some days it was quick. Other days, it seemed to drag on forever. There was a long, steep hill leading to town from the North. Driving down that hill was often treacherous, but no more so than during those months of unrest. To the north of town was a bridge that crossed the Kootenai River just outside of town. There were armed guard posted before the bridge, stopping cars and checking to make sure that those of us known to be of "Indian" blood had our armbands on.

Some of the guards knew our family and were friendly and kind, and we visibly agitated others. Those were the guards that struck fear into my heart. Sitting in the back of the car, panic would start to overcome me as men with snarling faces approached the car, guns in hand, to check us.

During the unrest, tensions grew between the "Indians" and the whites. Playing at recess, my friends became fewer and fewer, until one day, I heard my name being called, I turned to look, and I was knocked to the ground by a boy my age. His friends stood around and laughed, spewing racial slurs. I could not believe what was happening. My head was spinning.

Anger began to root itself deep in my belly. I could feel its burning need to get some repayment for the wrongs being done to me. I struggled to get up. Before I could get to my feet, I heard that guttural sound digging from inside his own gut and saw his lips purse as he coughed up enough phlegm to send spit flying my way. "Filthy Indian!" he growled. No one seemed to care to do anything. Laughing and taunting, they stood by and laughed until I got back to my feet preparing to swing. Then an adult stepped in to break it up.

Every day at school grew more and more volatile after that until it was implicitly unsafe for any of us "Indians" to be on school grounds. Even the adults did not seem to care much to protect us. Our best bet was not to even go to school.

*" Remember that your children are not your own,
but are lent to you by the Creator."*
Mohawk

For a short period of time during that unrest, we could not attend public school. We were sent to the tribal offices where all the "Indian" kids who had not stayed home were kept and corralled. The office was right downtown nestled in between businesses like JC

Penney and the local hardware store. There was not much studying going on—more playing and rambunctiousness, listening to music, and chasing each other through the offices. There were babies not even walking yet ranging in ages all the way up through teenagers.

It was chaotic with kids running all around the offices. I loved babies, so I gladly took over the duties of watching one round-faced little baby that was left there for the day.

Laughter, screeches, and giggles mixed with the sounds of furniture scraping across the floor as kids ran into desks and chairs. We were all aware of the tension outside and in the town, but we felt safe there in the offices with each other, oblivious to all that was going on around us.

Standing at the edge of a large, cold, grey metal desk, holding the baby on the edge, I was immersed in a different world for a moment playing with her and listening to her little laugh.

A thundering boom immediately followed by the sound of shattering glass came rushing through the room. Someone screamed in panic, "Get down! They are shooting!" Adults ran through pushing children to the ground in attempt to protect them. It was so surreal. Time seemed to stand still, and for a moment I did not move. I could not believe that this was happening in our small town, in my small life. Another resounding scream of "Get down!" rang through, and I shook loose of my frozen state of shock, grabbed the baby and ducked under the metal desk cowering in fear and disbelief.

I don't know how long we stayed hunkered under that desk, trembling in fear. Thoughts of bullets speeding through and visions of blood-spattered children ran through my mind. I was so terrified and sickened. These people in town had been our friends! What had I or any of these kids done wrong?

We were born with "Indian" blood and for that our lives meant nothing? We could be slaughtered without a second thought?

LIFTED UP

Eventually we were cleared to come out of hiding and a head count was taken. Thankfully, no one was hurt.

Like a landslide of rock and clay bearing down on our young souls, the realization that we were in a war with our own country, our community, neighbors, and church came crashing in on us that day. It was suffocating to think of all the people who once smiled and laughed with us, who now scorned us, spit at us, and SHOT at us!

My mind reeled. I had faced racism before in my young life, but not to that extreme. My heart sank as I began to sort through the pieces of wrong thinking. I acknowledged the same people who called us friends and prayed with us in church and were speaking against these things were the same ones committing the atrocities against us. These atrocities were based in anger and fear because of the color of our hair and skin and our heritage.

"How smooth must be the language of the whites, when they can make right look like wrong, and wrong like right."
Black Hawk, Sauk

Dad worked on the rebuilding of the old reservation outside of town. He cleared the roads and helped with improvements getting the land ready for the new houses to be built. Both my parents did the best they could to keep us involved with the Native side of our heritage.

Pow Wows were both wonderous and confusing for me. Dad and I loved to go! I loved to watch the dancing, hear the drums and the singing, see the bright colors, smell the fresh cooked fry bread, and hear the bells jingling as dancers stepped and pranced on the dusty earth. Dad's eyes would sparkle as he took my hand and led me to the stick games. Watching the hand movements in awe, he would laugh at me and try to explain the game to me as my eyes darted about trying to take in all that was going on.

My soul always felt so alive and warm, but at the same time so out of place. I was after all a "half breed". Back then; in the late 1960's and through the 1970's, it was a horrible thing to be called. It meant that the white men despised you, and yet the Native relatives often disowned you for not being a "pureblood".

I was sent to a camp with the Kootenai kids. I was so happy and excited to go because it meant being with my people. These were western Natives, and their skin very dark and faces round. I looked different to them because our tribe had more angular features, and my skin not so dark.

Knowing that I was mixed blood, they would torment me and make sure that I knew I was unpure and not good enough to be with them. What was meant to be a welcome respite from the unrest around us plunged me further into that space of "not enough". I was not the right skin color for either side.

"He rocks in the tree tops all day long
Hoppin' and a-boppin' and singing his song
All the little birdies on Jaybird Street
Love to hear the robin go tweet tweet tweet"
Michael Jackson

My solace during that week at camp with the dark-skinned kids was Michael Jackson! His song "Rockin Robin" had just come out, and just

hearing it made me happy and took me away to a happy space for a while. It was actually one place I was able to find commonality with the other kids.

It was not the first time I faced being shunned for my bloodline, nor would it be the last.

To compound that, sometimes it seemed that Mom wanted me to be Native, and other times she seemed ashamed of it. She made me an emerald green velvet dress to dance in. I loved that dress and was so proud to wear it. When I was alone, I would go find where it was hidden and put it on to dance in all by myself and think about my ancestors - the moccasins who walked this land before me.

Sometimes she would even dye my hair, so I would look more Native. Other times I would be forbidden to dance, as if I should be ashamed or she was ashamed of me. I did not understand at all and became so confused. In my heart, it did not matter what anyone else said, I was and am proud to be Native. My dad and my beloved grandpa were Native, and I was a part of them. No one could take that away from me.

"We do not want churches because they will teach us to quarrel about God. We do not want to learn that. We may quarrel with men sometimes about things on this earth, but we never quarrel about the Great Spirit. We do not want to learn that.
Chief Joseph

There was a period of time that Dad did not talk much about our heritage. Growing up for him meant being taken from his parents and put into Catholic school, braids cut off, and beatings for speaking his native tongue or anything to do with his heritage.

The Nuns and society taught him that to be Native was a bad thing. He was constantly in trouble at that school because he was so defiant. In those days, "Indian" lives were worth less than cattle, and murders happened and went unpunished.

There was great unrest between the Native tribes and our government when I was a child. Danger for us was very real.

In 1975, two Federal Agents drove into a compound in South Dakota where elders along with activists were holding a sweat lodge. They came in unannounced and opened fire, and as a result they were killed. It is important to note that they did not identify themselves as they came storming into the area guns drawn. There were many Native lives that were being taken, some mysteriously, during that time of unrest.

" Pine Ridge was a grim place, poor and depressed and ruled with an iron hand by government agents and Native American thugs. Peltier and the other defendants were members of the militant American Indian Movement (AIM), which two years earlier had taken over the Wounded Knee memorial site to draw attention to the plight of Native Americans and the conditions on the reservation. The FBI, stung by the acquittal of the other two defendants, wanted to make sure that Peltier was convicted. Witnesses who testified against Peltier say they lied because the FBI threatened and intimidated them. Evidence was withheld at the trial."
TCM.com

In the end, our cousin Leonard Peltier went on trial for the murders. The government had tried several others failing to gain convictions.

LIFTED UP

To this day, our people claim that it was a government set up to make sure someone answered for the crimes. Leonard was the last chance for them to do so. He is still in prison today. We still believe that he was wrongfully accused.

There have been multiple appeals and calls for pardon, but all have gone unanswered. I feel like Leonard is our own Mandela. Leonard was far from perfect, but to us it's obvious he is a token sacrifice by our government.

It amazes me how many people know nothing of many of these events or the eugenicide committed against our people during the 1970's and 1980's by our government. Our nation's leadership has kept some things well hidden from the general population.

Forty years ago, it really did feel like the wild west regarding many of these instances of murder, rape, social injustice, and the local, state and national government turning a blind eye to what was going on.

Even though I have witnessed some things in my lifetime, it is nothing compared to what my father and grandfather endured in the early 1900's in their own homeland.

With this in mind I wanted my children to grow up knowing some of their history. We lived a very different life than many of our relatives because we did not live near a reservation, but I still wanted them to know.

I started to teach them what I could and passed down stories from my dad and grandpa. We spent time with other teachers who helped us learn spiritual ways and carry them forward, including the sweat lodge.

Sweat lodge is a sacred place to pray and connect to our ancestors and Mother Earth. It is meant to mimic a womb, complete darkness inside. A place of extreme heat and suffering to cleanse us of negativity.

MISHA FAYANT

It was already a hot summer day, sweat dripping down our faces and backs as we gathered in the Northern Idaho woods. My two kids were young and busy playing with the other kids who gathered in the forest that day. Laughter filled the air.

The adults paired up and walked out into the woods in search of the perfect materials to build our lodge for that day. Hauling back the willow sapling branches we began to construct the lodge, bending the branches into the shape for the lodge around the pit that had been dug in the middle. Once we had tied the inverted bowl like structure and were satisfied with its size and shape, blankets were laid over top, layer by layer, taking care to leave no cracks where light could seep through. The inside of the lodge is meant to be dark, to heighten our inward awareness, mimic the womb of the Mother Earth, and keep distraction at bay.

Circling the structure, we checked every surface and made sure that not even the edges by the ground were loose to let light in. Though we were happy by that time we were all hot, covered in smoke and dust and sticky from our own sweat. Only when it was complete did we stop to rest, get water, and connect with everyone who was in attendance.

Approximately 20 feet away, stones were placed in a heap and covered with logs. A fire was started over these rocks and burned for hours, heating the rocks through. The smell of wood burned smoke drifted through the air. The heat from the mid-day sun was intensified by the mound of heating rocks.

With the structure of the lodge constructed and the rocks heating, we gathered the children to make prayer bundles. Scraps of bright red cloth were distributed to us all including the children. Tobacco was given to us as well. A pinch of tobacco was taken and prayed on, then gently placed in the center of the red cloth. Being careful to not let any of the tobacco escape, we then tied the cloth into small bundles. Another pinch of tobacco was taken for the next prayer, and the process repeated till our prayers were all contained in the

LIFTED UP

cloth. Once all our prayers were tied up in our bundles, we hung them from nearby trees while we built a smaller second fire.

The sun was just starting to set over the mountains, but the air was still hot and dry. Singing began, and we reverently took our bundles to the fire and dropped them in, allowing the fire to release the prayers in the tobacco and be carried to the Great Spirit in the smoke that drifted out of the fire. It is a very special and sacred moment watching those prayers rise into the sky, offered up for many differing reasons, some for our ancestors, some for health, or for family, etc.

The medicine man conducting the lodge then came and called us all to gather in one big circle. He began to speak and pray and give thanks to the 7 directions, North, West, South, East, Above, Below, and Within. Once this was done, the heated and glowing red stones that had been kept under searing hot fire were carried into the lodge by a special helper. One by one we were allowed to enter the lodge, entering and moving in a counterclockwise direction. We began taking our seats on the cool bare earth. Cross legged, we took our spots.

By the time the kids and I went in, we were building a second row around the circle, and the lodge was now hot from the radiant heat of the stones. It was so hot that entering the lodge took your breath away. This was not a time for talk. It was a time to be quiet. Keeping the kids – not just mine, but all that entered – quiet was a task. Once in, the flap to the entrance was closed, and we sat in complete darkness. The heat so intense, we were almost instantly drenched in sweat again, laboring to catch breath.

The medicine man began the prayer rounds, praying, and singing, tossing herbs or flowers onto the hot rocks, and occasionally splashing water over them to create steam and release the effects of the herbs. Round by round we prayed, clearing the space, inviting the ancestors in, sending out our prayers, and thanking them for their presence and help before sending them on again.

The process took hours, but it was filled with prayer and singing and the passing of a pipe. The kids held on as long as they could, but at one point my daughter started to feel panic and laid by the edge of the lodge trying to get air from the bottom where the blankets touched the ground.

The heat is intense, and meant for suffering, to give back for all that is given to us. A woman on her menses is never allowed in the lodge, because the act of losing blood during this time IS her suffering to give back. In the past, women were not allowed into a sweat lodge because we already give back every month, and the lodge was the place for the men to be silent, suffer, and give back.

Once the lodge ceremony was done and everyone had exited, we shared in a meal with the medicine men who gave us the opportunity to have sweat lodge. One lone plate was set out, with food and drink as an offering to the ancestors who came to help us that day.

There were native and Caucasian people alike at these lodges. It was so good to see some healing begin between the peoples. Many did not understand that it is customary to bring offerings to the men who give of their time and effort to bring us sweat lodge. We did our best to educate them for future lodges. The kids and I did not have much, but we brought some cash, tobacco, and food as our offering, which was gratefully accepted by these men who traveled from Central Washington to provide this opportunity for us.

I loved those days of work and prayer, suffering and song. It made me feel so connected to the ancestors that I know watch over me every day, who guide me and give me strength through each phase of life. This connection held me together through so many times of despair.

When things got tough, I would pause to think of all they had endured, all that my Dad had endured, and know that I could not fail. It was in my blood to get up and to continue to move forward through every trial, because of the strength that they emulated for me and the generations to come. The pride and love for not just humans, but the earth and all its creatures kept me centered.

For a time, I made crafts to sell at local fairs - medicine pouches, beadwork, flutes, moccasins, dreamcatchers, and a variety of other items centered around my culture. Most events were filled with respectful people, people who were intrigued and wanted earnestly to learn more, but occasionally there were the racial slurs that came crashing in. At one event, a mountain man came through and attempted to destroy my work, repeating all the slurs from my childhood and telling me how worthless my life and people were.

I had been working in a sewing factory, and it fell on hard times forcing the owners to close its doors in the spring just as school let out for the summer.

I decided it was a good time to spend the summer in adventure with the two kids and me - an escape from the home life I dreaded and to a connection I needed.

We started in Central Washington, in Yakima territory, attending Pow Wow and celebration, visiting sacred sites, and learning about different tribal cultures. Armed with a copy of "Indian Country" - a magazine detailing Pow Wows across the nation - we headed out on our summer long adventure. Each weekend a different Pow Wow moving from West eastward to the home of our tribe in the Turtle Mountains of North Dakota.

I had an old Ford Taurus wagon in forest green with a sunroof. We packed that old wagon to the gills with us, our regalia, food, tents, supplies, and headed out. We used the winnings I made from dancing to take us across the country.

It was a magical time for us all. Each Pow Wow we stopped at was filled with elders that took time to share and teach us about their tribe and customs, and children who came to sit and listen to storytelling by me.

MISHA FAYANT

"Why we dance;
To dance is to pray,
To pray is to heal,
To heal is to give,
To give is to live,
To live is to dance."
Marijo Moore

There were no cell phones, no computers, just us, and creation and relatives everywhere we went. The sound of drums filled our days and nights. The hot sweet smell of fry bread enticed us every weekend. There was no air conditioning to cool us, only the prairie breeze, or the big duck feathered fan I carried to dance. We lived simple for a summer, but we were together, and surrounded by people, relatives from many nations across, Washington, Idaho, Montana, and North Dakota.

My dress was traditional buckskin; the hem followed the natural contour of the leather it was made from. I went against the trends toward modernism and made my regalia traditional. Over top of the buckskin dress, I wore a black velvet cape that was beaded with traditional Ojibwa designs. My moccasins were made as my tribe made them for centuries, with a puckered seam up the middle instead of the prairie seam to the side. My leggings were a soft supple natural cream buckskin. My waist was adorned with a thick leather belt, from which hung a bag made from a turtle shell, with buckskin sewn to the back and a flap beaded with traditional design. Another bag hung from my waist of green velvet with the woodland flowers embroidered on it, a long leather strap hung to one side. I wore a bone necklace tied around my throat and a large heavy draped necklace I made from black bone beads and old trader style cobalt beads. My fan was made from a duck wing I had found alongside the road and salvaged what I could in honor of its life. In my hair, attached with a woodland beaded hairpiece, stood a lone eagle feather in honor of my father. I had two shawls - an old orange wool shawl (from my childhood) and a newer pink one with long fringes that swayed rhythmically with my steps.

I felt so regal and proud when I stepped into that dress. I danced traditional style, and often I wished that I could dance jingle style or fancy, but they were fast paced and exhausting! My dress was heavy, many days it took care just to stay upright and not topple over if a misstep was made on the uneven ground we danced on.

I had made my kids regalia as well, and they danced with the other kids and during Grand Entry. My daughter's dress was black velvet with woodland style loom beaded bands across the hem and sleeves. My son wore a traditional woodland breech cloth, black velvet, long in front and back, with buckskin leggings and a bone breast plate. He also wore a head piece of fur and horns to resemble the buffalo, that headpiece was nearly as wide as he was tall.

We have so many stories and memories of those days of Pow Wows and dancing. Each tribe we visited brought new memories and experiences. In North Dakota nearing home, we stopped at a Hidatsa dance. There an elder lady found me, gave me a nod of approval for my regalia, then grabbed my hand and took me into the circle to dance. She grinned a weathered, bright smile and quietly said, "Watch this, and follow me."

She proceeded to dance in a style I had not seen before. Round and round the circle we went until I mastered the footsteps she was showing me. At the end of the night, she took my arm once again and pulled me aside. "I do not show others my steps," she said. "But you carry the ancestors with you, and you honor them with your dress, and so I give you this gift." Her smile melted my heart, her touch reached into my soul, and I felt transported, as if taken to a circle of ancestors and elders where I sat with them in communion.

I never felt at ease with those my own age. I always felt far more connected to the elders, and they must have felt it, too, because every stop was filled with stories of elders who took me aside to teach me something. I am so honored by these blessings.

"Being an Indian is an attitude, a state of mind, a way of being in harmony with all things and all beings. It is allowing the heart to be the distributor of energy on this planet; to allow feelings and sensitivities to determine where energy goes; bringing aliveness up from the Earth and from the Sky, putting it in and giving it out from the heart. "
Brooke Medicine Eagle

LIFTED UP

CHAPTER 5

WHY CAN'T YOU BE MORE LIKE HER?

"Dear Mom,
I'm sorry I couldn't make you any prouder of me,
I'm sorry I didn't turn out the way
you wanted me to be,
I'm sorry that I'm a disappointment to you."
Unknown

It was Easter Sunday. I was up early and quietly made my way to the dining room where, to my excitement, I found baskets full of goodies sitting on the table. I snuck up and read the tags. There were baskets for my cousins, but nothing for me. I was confused. Mom must have just forgotten to put my basket out. When she finally woke and came to the kitchen, I nervously followed her. It was clear she was yet again annoyed with me. Her voice took on that sharp edge that made my spine tingle. "What do you want?" she barked at me.

"Mommy, I was just wondering where my basket is? I see baskets for everyone else, even my cousins, but I cannot find mine," I replied sheepishly.

LIFTED UP

Her eyes rolled, and now I knew she was annoyed at me. She looked at me sternly and said, "You're such a selfish little brat. Your cousins don't have much, so I bought baskets for them. You have more than they do, so you did not need one."

Needless to say, I was crushed. As an adult it seems like such a small thing, but it was just one more in a progression of me not being recognized. My cousin was blonde haired, blue eyed, and thin—all the things I was not. I was reminded of that nearly daily. She was the one who seemed could do no wrong. She was taken on as a "daughter" by Mom, replacing me in one fell swoop. It was not my cousin's fault. She was the same age as me—how could she know what was happening!

The fact is, it was crushing for my young, little soul. It was a clear message to my child's mind that I was not wanted. No matter how hard I tried, I could never measure up to what she was capable of. I spent years trying—years jumping up and down, trying to be the good girl, trying to do all the things I thought were expected of me so that I could gain my mother's love back from my cousin and once again be my mother's daughter.

She was everybody's favorite, and I was the awkward one. Her family moved back to Montana by the time we were teenagers. I loved her. She was my cousin. Of course, I looked up to her. She was all that I never could be according to my mom. Still I tried.

When she began having issues as a teenager, I will admit I found some odd solace in the fact that the cracks were showing. She was, in fact, just as imperfect as me. I hoped I would regain my seat as daughter when things began to come out about her imperfection. Instead, I was pushed further away. After all, she needed love and attention more than ever.

Each year that passed, I found myself coveting her spot in life, wanting to be her, to be seen and heard, and forgiven unconditionally. It was not a healthy place to be, but it had become part of my story. The messages of "you're not enough" that were delivered to me in everyother corner of life solidified themselves in this arena. I could not even be a worthy daughter.

One summer, we all headed out to church camp held in the south center of Montana. I have always tried to find the bright side of things, and so I rushed forward into life believing that somehow, some way I would be enough one day.

At the end of camp, there was an award given each year for the young man and woman who most represented Nazarene values. The other campers voted on it. Sitting in the mess hall, laughing with my friends, a huge part of my heart screamed out that I wished I could win that award. Maybe, just maybe, if I won that award, I would be recognized and accepted by Mom. Just as soon as the thought went through my head, I started to push it aside, remembering, "I am not enough. No one wants to see me." Still I was smiling and joking with my friends about who it may be who was chosen.

"Dear YOU, don't compare yourself to ANYONE. Your Unique Self is empowered, powerful, and unstoppable! Your uniqueness is what makes you incomparable! Don't underestimate the beauty of just being YOU."
Stephanie Lahart

The moment came when they were announcing the name of Miss Northwest Nazarene. We all became suddenly silent. The speaker called out a name, but I could not hear it. A silence fell over my ears that made me feel deaf in an instant. My friends began nudging cheering and me. I was still shocked—the name that had been called was MINE! Wearing a satiny, pale pink dress, I walked down

LIFTED UP

the aisle to the pinnacle of the party that evening with my handsome male counterpart who had been chosen. The evening was magical and felt like a scene from Cinderella. I was seen and acknowledged by everyone there. Now Mom would see me for sure!

The trophy presented to me during the gala now seemed foolish and unnecessary when presented to Mom. The love and accolades I had hoped and longed for were replaced with indifference. Beaming with pride, I had excitedly shown my prize. I was the only one at home who was proud of me. It was as if I was selfish for "showing it off".

The trophy stood on my dresser for a while, my reminder of a bliss that came when others that I barely knew found value in me. Eventually, it was tucked away in a large green travel trunk with my other treasures—a symbol, a physical reminder that I could indeed be seen, and I could be enough.

The battle to be Mom's daughter, Mom's pride and joy, continued on into adulthood. Even when I thought it as just a figment of my childish imagination, the dysfunctional relationship and competition with my cousin would come back to haunt me.

For a time, she lived in the same town as Mom, having married a man whose family owned a business there. I was happy to see her. She had such a bright smile.

Without warning, the darkness of comparison and never being enough began to roll in. They owned a nice home in town, and she worked doing the books for the business. She had a respectable job, and what had I done? I gave up. It would never change no matter what I did. The story would always be skewed in her favor.

In the age of computers and Facebook, I was reminded yet again of my inadequacy and nonexistence. Posts were made by Mom talking about her children, only I was never mentioned anywhere in them. In my place, love and adoration was given to my cousin. One post even mentioned how she was "the daughter she always wished she had".

I know that our relationship had its ups and downs and that I had not been a perfect daughter, but those things crushed my soul. Just when I thought I was healing from this corner of my life, the wounds would be ripped open.

Depression followed. That old prayer of wanting to be dead would take over. Darkness would fall over me. Tears and hidden breakdowns filled my life and mind. Pieces of me shattered away each time I was compared to her and told, "why can't you be more like her." It was a task I would never be able to attain.

"When we accept the labels placed on us by ourselves and others, we then restrict and limit ourselves based on those labels. Break free from them and reclaim your unlimited potential to be your amazing self."
Nanette Mathews

LIFTED UP

CHAPTER 6

INFIDELITY AND DIVORCE

"There are all kinds of ways for a relationship to be tested, even broken, some, irrevocably; it's the endings we're unprepared for."
Katherine Owen

Adorned in green denim covered in embroidered farm figures, I stood in our driveway holding Daddy's hand. Filled with pride, I stood tall. Mom had spent so long making this outfit for me, I wore it every chance I could. Adult voices said their goodbyes. Janet and Burton, our neighbors, were leaving from a family visit.

Manners were different then. We walked visitors to their cars and said goodbyes to them as they entered their vehicle. Watching until they drove away, we would wait before returning to our home.

The Spring afternoon sun was still shining. Pappa's laughter and smooth, deep voice filled my ears, and I looked up to see his bright smile and shining eyes. The best days of my life were standing by his side. I felt protected, loved, needed, wanted, and seen.

LIFTED UP

My name. I heard my name. Daddy was asking me to go find my mother. There was nervous agitation in his voice. It was so impolite for her not to be there to say goodbye. He did not have to speak another word. I knew what he was saying.

His grip on my hand softened, and then pushed toward the house behind us. Uh oh! Go! Turning, my feet moved as quickly as they could, up and down the stairs into the house searching for Mom.

It was not much of a search. There were only two doors in the unfinished basement we lived in, one on my brothers' bedroom door and one on the bathroom door.

Darting in and out of the open spaces, I called "Mom!" But she was nowhere to be seen. The bathroom door was closed. Butterflies filled my stomach as I gently knocked on the door. I did not want to upset her, but I had been sent on a mission.

No answer. Just a soft groan.

"Mom!?" I called out again.

Nothing but the still soft groan from the other side of the door. Butterflies turned into something heavier like maggots writhing in the pit of my gut. Ear pressed against the door, every nerve on notice, I listened. She was in there, but why did she not answer?

The soft groan turned into something sharper, more urgent—a small muffled cry of pain.

That's it! I flung the door open, and I tumbled into the expansive bathroom. Mom's body slumped over the small step up in the bathroom floor, one hand grasping, holding to the sink cabinet.

As she lifted her head, the face looking back at me sent chills through me—gaunt, pale, sunken, eyes dull and filled with pain, almost pleading. A gasp fell from my mouth. What happened to my mom? The woman in front of me looked 20 years older, frail, and on death's door. Panic and confusion clumsily bumped through my skull.

I scanned the room, begging for answers, and saw her hand grasping her belly. Something was horribly wrong!

Feet running, heart pacing faster, I went outside again.

"Pappa! Something's wrong!" I screamed out as soon as the sun touched my skin exiting the house.

He turned and looked at me confused and clearly angry. Our neighbors said quick goodbyes as Pappa and I stormed the house down the stairs to where she still lay on the floor.

Without pause, he bent down to scoop her up like a rag doll, barking orders for me to grab the pickup keys and her purse and get outside. Done! Breath quickening and body numbing, I ran out the door once again down the gravel drive to find Pappa stuffing her quickly and gently into the truck seat.

Meeting him on the passenger side, I handed him the keys and purse. One foot on the tire, the other leg swung over the truck bed, body tumbling into it, my position was posted next to the opening in the rear window, so I could keep an eye on her as we drove.

Laughter and raucous came crashing across the wooded yard from my two brothers who didn't seem to recognize the gravity of the situation.

"We are taking Mom to the hospital! C'mon!" I screamed as the pickup engine fired up.

"Nah, we don't want to go!" I was shocked to hear my brothers' reply. What? Not going? Mom is sick! Really sick!

No time to respond, the pickup was tossing gravel, behind it as the

LIFTED UP

engine growled, and we sped out of the drive. The 6-mile trip to the hospital seemed never ending. Shivering from the spring air combined with the terror filing my core as I watched her face become more gaunt and sunken.

Tires screaming, the pickup stormed the front entrance of the hospital. I had never seen Pappa move so quickly. Before I could get up and out of the truck bed, he had already opened the passenger door, extracted her from her seat, and was headed to the entry doors.

Inside was a blur. Hospital lights, shouts, nurses and doctors. Pappa's commanding voice was quivering. My post was taken in a cold, narrow waiting room chair. Legs up then down, fetal position, then throwing themselves out as if to run, but to where? Time stood sickeningly still as we waited to hear if she was okay or if she was even alive.

Answers finally came as a doctor stepped out to give Pappa the news. She had a tubal pregnancy that burst and caused internal bleeding. If we had arrived 5 or 10 more minutes later, we would have certainly lost her. I heard soft voices muffled that I could not make out, and then the doctor nodded to me a compassionate look and quietly said, "You saved her life, young lady."

Relief! I may not have understood the dynamic of our relationship, but I loved her so much. The ride home was much warmer as I sat in the passenger seat, most of the concern lifted from my conscience. We would go back in the morning to retrieve her after she was observed overnight.

Soon it was time to go get Mamma and bring her home! The boys were still not interested in the trip. They just wanted to hang out at home and play. Once again, Pappa and I made the trek.

Pulling up to the hospital, love and joy filled my heart. I had saved her life. I showed her how much I loved her! I had been there when her beloved boys were not. It had to mean something and had to give me a place in her heart to accept me. Today would be my day! Now she had to know how much I loved her, and she would return that to me with thanks and acknowledgement. I was all of about 13 years old.

Pacing, staring at the grey, shiny floor of the hospital, I waited for her to be brought out. Lost in the sight of my feet moving, one, two, one, two, across that cold floor, I heard my name. Swiftly, my head turned, eyes searching for my parents, smile breaking across my face and love flooding my heart, I saw them coming toward me. Mom was in a wheel chair. I moved toward them, wanting to give her a hug and tell her how much I loved her.

To my dismay, her arm swept out and shoved me away. Looking into her eyes and wanting to see love, I found deep seething anger instead. I was confused! What now? What had happened? The doctor said I did good. I saved her life! How could she be mad at me?

Shrinking into that oh-so-familiar invisibility cloak I had woven for myself, I shrank away to the truck and waited. Once out of earshot of the hospital staff, she looked at me with so much anger; it sent a chill down my spine. Begging for approval, my eyes met hers.

"I hate you!
I will never forgive you for this."

"I hate you! I will never forgive you for this! Do you hear me? I will never forgive you! You should have let me die! Why do you always meddle? Leave me alone." Venom spewed forth and seared my soul eating away until it was numb. The bite of the cold air meant nothing on the trip home. Curled up in the truck bed, knees tucked to my head, I sobbed until my face was flooded with salty tears. Trembling, every inch of me covered in a numb but stinging pain, I felt lost.

Thoughts of jumping out of the moving truck bed and finding sweet relief from this life crowded the empty spots in my thoughts. Nothing I ever did was right or was enough. My heart shattered into shards all over that truck bed floating away in a river of tears.

But, Pappa! I could not hurt him like that. He loved me. He would be so hurt if I did that. He had been through enough. He would never forgive me or understand. The only choice left was to suck it up and continue. His love was enough for both of them. He did not hate me. It was time to be the strong girl he raised and live another day.

I had no idea at the time what was going on and why she was so angry.

"The mother's heart is the child's schoolroom."
Henry Ward Beecher

Years later I would find out that Pappa had been fixed after my younger brother was born. It was not just my birth that gave her trouble. He was born early, and there were severe health issues for her during the pregnancy and delivery. Pappa had made the decision to have a vasectomy to prevent any future issues. That was 12 years earlier!

Ah, the ignorance of youth. Mindset so ingrained in our church upbringing and the good Christian family that was her side of the lineage, I had no inkling of what our life was really entwined in. Both my parents had affairs, and she was caught! Everyone knew that Pappa could not have any more children, which meant that the spotlight glared on her for the affair that seeded the now aborted baby she had been carrying.

Battles followed. It was the beginning of the battlefield that became the next decades of our lives.

Mom, too proud, embarrassed, and scared to admit that she had an affair insisted that the child was Dad's. She demanded tests be taken. Proof was needed that his vasectomy had been faulty, and he was indeed the father of the child. That story was frantically pushed through our tiny Northern Idaho community. Results solidified the fact that he could not be the father. Our world did not crumble. It imploded.

Stuck smack in the middle of the conflict, my mental state began to erode. Mild discomfort in my belly turned into burning pain, and then I began spitting up blood.

Grandma's house! That was the answer, I was shipped away to Montana to live with Grandma and go to school there.

Healing sat juxtaposed to increased worry. So far from the reach of the insanity that was home, I felt loved and sheltered for the first time in quite a while. Grandma made all of us grandkids feel like we were the "special" one.

Quilting, cooking, and laughter filled our days as she tried so desperately to save me from the corrosion she saw deep in my soul.

Being transferred to a new school and plopped headlong into new curriculum compounded my already fragile mental state. Making friends was not easy. I had grown so used to being the awkward, unseen outcast.

My stomach improved, but other things began unplugging from my

LIFTED UP

internal wiring. Mentally things were a blur. Inside I felt like a crater falling in on itself after a lava flow. Walking the halls of school, walls became a blur and the ground I walked on felt as if I was walking the deck of a ship at sea. Bang! My head crashed into the corner of a wall, landing me on my butt and almost knocking me out. After a few occurrences like that, it was decided to send me back home.

Deep emotion made way for an inlet of intuition. I had always seen images of scenes that would later come true. Those few months at Grandma's house in the quiet and peace, I began "seeing" with a high-pitched fever.

One recurring vision was of Dad walking into a truck stop, the glass storefront shining slivers of bright light across a long dark countertop. Padded stools spun on their bases lined the counter. A petite woman, with light curly hair and a crossed leg that kicked and fidgeted, sat with her side leaned into the bar. Her voice rang through the truck stop café. A thin line of smoke rose from the cigarette poised in her back-turned hand. She was the focus of the vision once in the door. Dad walked straight to her, and as he neared I could see her face, bright with a knowing smile. He leaned in, and their lips met in a lover's kiss. What the heck? This could not be!

Later that year I would meet her, and the vision would make eerie sense.

Back at home in Idaho, tension had escalated. Pappa spent increasingly more time away from home. Eventually, he rented a singlewide trailer in town, which was his place of respite.

Reality settled in about what had happened, and my mother's increased dislike of me convinced me to move from the still unbuilt house in the woods to live with Dad in the small trailer on the other side of town.

Evenings were quiet and peaceful, just Dad and me. For a moment, I felt the rush of fresh air in my lungs and soul. I did not know how to cook yet. Spaghetti was my go-to dish. It was all-good, but soon Pappa asked if I could come up with something else to fix for dinner as he was getting tired of spaghetti. Embarrassed, I began trying to learn other dishes to fix for him.

Dad seemed different. He was happy again and full of the life I remember. Just Dad and I, it was perfect! Then, in the dark of the night, Mom arrived, pouring on every ounce of charm she could muster. Between sweet remarks to Dad were glaring glances thrown my way.

The couch was my safe spot, or so it seemed. I sat frozen there, not wanting to move, staring at the glare from the television. Sooner than I would have thought, they ended up in Dad's room, but at least I had quiet again.

Mesmerized by the television, I barely heard the door open. Completely naked, she came strolling out triumphant as if she had just won something and began barking orders at me once again. What the heck just happened?

The boys moved in soon after, and it felt all too silly that we all had left a perfectly good home to end up in a trailer house in the KOA campground at the edge of town.

We were right back in the middle of the war zone. My older brother always had a chip on his shoulder, and his anger increased in that little trailer.

I think my younger brother had ADHD. He could not for the life of him sit still! He was always poking, prodding, and pestering us—anyone he could get to really.

Arriving home from school, there was some kind of horseplay going on and then quiet. Ah, I love the quiet. All too soon it ended, the sound of my younger brother screaming, drowned out by the

LIFTED UP

booming voice of my older brother threatening to kill him. Legs bounding as quick as I could, I ran to the back of the house, where Louis, the older, was holding Bob, the younger up by the neck with one hand and hitting him with the other over and over. Bob's legs frantically kicking and arms swinging to no avail.

"LOUIS, STOP!" I yelled with the most commanding voice I could muster.

He did not stop. "Suck it up, Chelle," the voice inside said, and wham, I punched him. Stunned, he turned and looked at me growling, still holding Bob—feet dangling in a chokehold. Bob's face was turning from red to an odd blue-purplish color.

"STOP!" I screamed again standing firm.

I heard Bob come thudding to the floor as Louis turned to me grasping for me. Now that Bob was released, I bolted just in time.

In that one instant, I realized how much my brothers were hurting in this situation, too. Scary does not even describe that moment in time. I had never stood up to Louis before. The mere thought of it struck fear in every cell of my being. It was the beginning of the end of our relationship as brother and sister.

It wasn't long before Dad could take no more of his relationship with Mom. Because he could not get her to move, he moved.

The trucking company he worked for was stationed in Southern Montana. He was often gone for long haul deliveries and returned home from time to time.

One night during that time, during a football game, family life came crashing back in once again to disrupt the escape I found when hanging out with friends.

Crowds cheering, the dark night lit by stadium lights, I sat in the bleachers with my friends, for an evening oblivious to the wreckage of my life. That did not last long. Midway into the game, I could hear gasps in the crowd around me. It felt as if the red sea was parting.

Crowd moving away in slow motion before my eyes, time slowed to a near halt as I watched her come toward me.

Hysterical, clothes ripped, an earring missing, and face stained with black rivers of mascara running down her cheeks, Mom came rushing toward me screaming, "He's gone mad! He's crazy! He tried to kill me! He's going to drive his truck off the Moyie Bridge! (The tallest bridge in the Northwest) You're not safe! None of us are safe! The police are looking for him! He tried to kill me!" So much horrible information was rushing at me all at once.

I was confused once again. This did not sound like Dad. He had a temper, but he would never lose it like this!

"Mom, what are you talking about?" I asked in terror.

"He's gone crazy! Look what he did to me! He tried to kill me! You can't go home. Go to a friend's house, and don't come home until I call you. It's not safe! Don't call just wait. Don't come home!"

Over and over she insisted that I could not go home until she or the police called me, and that under no uncertain terms was I to call home. (There were no cell phones back then.)

My friend, Tammi, lived down the gravel road and across the country highway from me. Her house is where I landed on that frightening night.

Nearly a week had gone by with no word from anyone. Too terrified to disobey Mom and call or go by the house, I spent most of my days in her basement bedroom crying and driving myself crazy with gruesome thoughts. Did I even have a family to go home to? Was my Dad alive? Was Mom alive? Where were my brothers, and were they alive? Visions of my entire family bloody and dead filled my head

LIFTED UP

and made my heart cry out. When I did leave her room, I spent most of my time staring at the phone as if willing it to ring.

Watching the news every day, I prayed there would be news of my family, and yet I hoped there would not be. No answers, no communication, my psyche was imploding. I would have rather been interned and tortured than go through another day not knowing what had happened to my family.

Tammi's mom finally had enough and commanded me to call the house. Soul screaming at the thought of Mom's anger at me for disobeying, my body quaked at the thought. Trembling so hard I could barely hold the phone much less dial, I called home. Holding my breath, unsure of what was about to happen, I waited as the phone rang.

"Hello!" The voice of my younger brother chimed across the phone line. Stunned I paused.

"Hello?" he said again.

"You're home? You're okay?" my reply must have amused him.

He began laughing like an imp and replied, "Of course! Why?"

My heart stuck in my throat as I found the will to ask, "How long have you been home?"

He was clearly confused and irritated by my questions. I finally found that he and my older brother had been home all along, unaware of the trauma. All was well.

That old familiar feeling of waves crashing across the shore of my mind came rumbling through as I began heaving, holding back the vomit that was insisting on finding its way out. Why?! Why did she do this to me? Why was I tortured so? Why did no one even notice that I was gone? So many questions. The cloak of invisibility gained a solid lining that day. I knew now that I was not wanted, not needed, and not even missed by my family.

Still sick from the reality, I gathered my things to make the walk home. That quarter-mile of road seemed endless, as my feet drug through the gravel. One more brick was added in the unseen, unwanted, never enough structure that I lived in.

Home felt like a horror show. I did not feel safe. It was no longer about being unwanted, I had premonition of not being safe.

Within a year, Mom was pregnant again.

"It's not that difficult, I want to say. People cheat all the time.
The reasons are always selfish and base, it's the excuses
we make that are complicated."
Sarah Pinborough

LIFTED UP

CHAPTER 7

LIVING WITH PAPPA

"Being a daddy's girl is like having permanent armor
for the rest of your life."
Marinela Reka

Pappa had begun working for a trucking company in Great Falls Montana and moved to escape the chaos of the marriage that was inevitably ending.

The small brown station wagon that was my escape pod made it through the precarious mountain roads between Idaho and Montana. Music blared Rod Stewart and my untuned voice blared even louder as my joy grew the closer I drew to Great Falls.

No cell phones, just a map and some hand-written directions with an address led me to my destination. Expansive and flat compared to home, the city felt strange and yet ripe with adventure.

Roads long and straight defined the outskirts of town where the truck stops backed up to trailer courts. This is where I found my destination. Pulling up to the entrance of the rows of singlewide trailers, the manager's trailer was to the left.

Still full of energy from the excitement of my escape, even after driving several hundred miles, I bounded up the wooden ramp to the door that held the "manager" sign. Quick short taps fell from my knuckles to the door in anticipation. Blonde, short, curly hair capped the head of the slight figure answering the tin door. Why did she seem so familiar?

"I'm looking for Louis Fayant's trailer," my voice cracked as the words came out.

A knowing smile swept across the tiny woman's face as she relayed the information about which space, the color, and location of the trailer I was looking for.

I hopped back in the brown wagon and drove to the back of the park where I found Pappa's pickup truck parked. She had given me the key, as he had instructed her that I was coming, and I would need to get in.

That trailer seemed like a castle to me. Pushing through the front door, I explored the layout of my new home. Furnishings were sparse, just as I expected. After all, it was the new home of a trucker man. A man who found home base there but did not spend much time there.

It did not take long to unload my few belongings and tuck them away in their new spaces.

"One of the greatest gifts I've ever gotten came from God.
I call him Daddy."

The air, though dry and hot, felt so fresh and clean. I stood in the middle of that small but wide-open living room, arms outstretched and twirled until my head spun taking in the feeling of freedom, safety, and pure joy. Dusk was just beginning to fall when I heard his voice as he walked up the path to our home. My legs could not move quick enough to get to the door and welcome him home!

Hugs, laughter, and those sparkling blue eyes met me as the door flung open. Pappa was always proud of his appearance, so he insisted on getting a shower right away. He was hot, tired, and dusty from the day of driving.

Cleaned up and donning blue slacks and a button down western shirt with brown boots peeking out underneath, he smiled and said, "Let's go get something to eat!"

A long glass front, low roofed diner sat across the road from the park. He took my hand as we chattered and walked toward our destination.

"Deja vu is one of the weirdest things that happens
to me. It boggles my mind. "
Chino Moreno

Déjà vu? I had a distinct feeling of knowing that building. I had seen it somewhere before. Opening the front door, it came flooding across me, as time slowed, and my mind caught up to the cues my heart and gut had been dishing up. Surreal does not begin to describe the feeling—more like stepping into a movie that you dreamed some time ago. Dreaming? Awake? Hold on, wait a minute I squeezed his hand. Yes, awake.

Sitting at the counter, I could see the back of a small woman, blonde hair, legs crossed, and one leg flicking about. She leaned up against the counter. Her hand tilted back at its wrist, and between her fingers

LIFTED UP

a cigarette burned, a wispy thin line of smoke danced up to the fan that sucked it away.

My stomach tensed. All the breath escaped from my lungs and did not return as I realized who and what this was. It was that dream, that vision I had many months before while living with Grandma. This was that diner. This was that woman! This was Pappa's new love.

His dark, weathered hand reached out and touched her shoulder, causing her to turn toward us. There was that smile I had seen. There was that kiss I witnessed. This was the woman from the trailer park!

That year, visions began coming in and coming true with ever increasing frequency.

That summer in Montana was all the adventure I had imagined it to be. Pappa was out driving most days. I had freedom! I had learned to cook and took pride in making even the simplest meal look fancy.

I used cookbooks filled with French recipes and wine. Lots and lots of wine filled my days.

Boredom settled in some days, but I had freedom! I had filled out physically earlier than most girls my age. Yes, I had breasts! All this meant I looked older than I was. I took trips to the store for groceries, and I felt so grown up, but never more so than when I discovered no one batted an eye when I threw wine in the cart. I wasn't even questioned!

This discovery opened the door for days of drunken gymnastics all alone in that sparse trailer living room. The wine gave me a bravery I had not felt before. Some days I listened to the radio as I drank and danced. I made calls to the radio station, harassing and flirting with the DJ and requesting Rod Stewart's "Do Ya Think I'm Sexy" more times than was reasonable.

I soon learned what a hangover was and what being miserably

drunk was. All afternoon cooped up in that house drinking and doing flips, cartwheels, leaps, and turns soon led to wobbly legs and an even wobblier head. Laughing, I stumbled to my bed.

My head spun uncontrollably. This was no longer fun! Oh my gosh, I was going to be sick! One, two, three trips to the bathroom crouched over the cold toilet. I focused enough to find a 5-gallon bucket and placed it by my bed. Eventually the night was spent with my head drooping over the edge of the bed, my face buried in the bucket retching over and over emptying the very depths of my belly in violent gushing rushes until I was finally empty.

Somewhere in the middle of the night, Pappa came home. Of course, he understood what happened. The trail of wine bottles, the mess in the living room, and the stench from the bucket by my bed told the entire story he needed to know.

That morning he was louder than normal, banging, clanging, slamming doors, singing, and laughing. Lesson learned!

Weekends meant going dancing with him and his newfound love. He taught me to play pool those summer nights and to drink something more than wine! More than one older man tried to make his way past Dad, soon learning the wrath of Pappa if they were inappropriate with his daughter. At the same time, his eyes sparkled, and he smiled. He was proud of his girl for getting so much attention. I felt pretty, I felt wanted, and I felt joy.

All too soon the summer ended, and with its end we packed up and moved back to Idaho, with the new woman and her daughter in tow. Our little rag tag caravan made its way from western Montana to Northern Idaho. This time though we settled in a town a few hours south of my hometown, and I was enrolled in a new school.

I still felt so out of place in my new school. All those years of not being enough came crashing back in, and I felt as if no one here wanted to be bothered with the new girl. To top it off, I was smart and a

LIFTED UP

good student. My hand was always up in response to teacher's questions. More than one teacher told me to put my hand down and let someone else answer. Conflict! My insides screamed, proud at being the only one to know the answers and yet embarrassed for being told to stop, feeling like once again I was not wanted to be seen.

Somehow, I was seen by a golden haired, vibrant wrestling jock. The one who would a few months later claim my virginity and leave me feeling dirty after finding out he lied about being broken up with the girl he had been seeing.

Wounds fresh from the traumas of divorce and the threats the random punishments from Mom had crushed my mental state. Nighttime meant terrors. Most nights I could not bear to go to sleep. I had nightmares of snakes everywhere—in my bed, in my car, under my feet. No matter where I stepped, they were ready to bite in any second. I had nightmares of being taken by a dog-man and raped over and over. I had nightmares of being chased by a mother who was trying to murder me.

"Personally, I have nightmares about the
unstoppable monster."
David Slade

Screams, panic, and fingers clawing at the wall. Sheetrock embedded under my nails as I frantically tried to break through the barrier in front of me trying to escape from the one coming with a blade to cut me into pieces and throw me away.

I woke to Pappa shaking me, tears in his eyes. He held me tight, rocking me, telling me it was okay. "Your safe, my girl, I have got you.

MISHA FAYANT

Daddy won't let anyone hurt you anymore." That night Pappa said he finally began to realize the hell I had been living in. Anger, frustration, and desperation coursed through his veins as he held my hands bleeding from the fingertips and staring at the wall that now bore my marks.

I heard him asking his new love what the hell had happened while he was gone to make me be so terrified. He drank, swore, and cried that night until we all fell back asleep.

That fall he married her, and she became my stepmom. He seemed so happy, and I wanted him to be happy.

She and I tried to get along, but the bond between Pappa and I ate away at her.

Our late arrival and enrollment in that school meant I missed out on the volleyball team. However, I got to play Basketball!

Concrete street courts and battling my way around the boys that were friends of my brothers the previous year, taught me to be a more aggressive player. I was more aggressive than the girls at the time were known to be.

Some games I almost fouled out, as I charged other girls. I played point guard. I wasn't the best shooter, but I could get the ball down the court!

In December, work and Pappa's desire to see his sons took us back to that Northern town of Bonner's Ferry. A friend and Kootenai tribal member had a home north of town that he rented to us.

It was a big home, big for me anyway, with two levels and four bedrooms. It had a living room upstairs and another downstairs. New furniture that Pappa bought for his new wife was placed throughout the house and we settled in.

LIFTED UP

I worked, bugged, and begged the basketball coach to let me on the team until I made it! Christmas break was spent integrating myself into the team, learning their plays, and getting re-acquainted with old friends. I forged my spot on the team.

I did not get to start our first game after the break. Coach did not feel it was fair since I arrived halfway through the season. A few minutes into the game, I hit the court though! Running up and down the court, my eyes darted to the crowd looking for my family.

My brothers were both athletes, and Mom made sure she went to all their games. Even with my fears and emotional trauma, I loved her. I longed for her acceptance. A part of me refused to feel whole until I could gain her acceptance and attention.

Pappa, Sinda (my stepmom), and Linda, (my new stepsister) sat in the bleachers behind our team. My brothers, Louis and Robert, were spotted in the bleachers with the rest of the kids on the other side of the court. Mom? Where was mom? I could not find her. Over and over, I scanned the crowds thinking she would be there. The whole rest of the family was there, but I never saw her. Pure heavy lead sat in the pit of my gut. Something was wrong!

Pulling into the driveway of our new home, Pappa noticed something wrong. Sinda screamed irrationally. Linda and I bolted for our rooms.

Clothing that I had just purchased was missing. Mementos from my now dead Auntie were missing. What I could not reconcile was the simple things... Gifts from Dad were shattered, pictures of Dad and I ripped in half and the half with him in it torn to shreds. Why? Rage, hurt, desperation—my familiar old friends came visiting once more. Was pain all the attention that I would ever receive from her?

Personal items were missing from Pappa and Sinda as well. The cake top from their wedding cake was gone, their wedding photos destroyed, and her wedding gown missing. It was obviously a personal attack and well thought out. That cake top (or one just like it) showed up on a wedding cake a few months later at Mom's wedding in Montana.

The clothes that were missing were found the next fall in the basement of her home tucked away, mixed in with other items. The day after I discovered them, they disappeared as if they were never there. I found pictures of Dad and the personal things he and Sinda were missing carefully hidden in shoe boxes tucked away in the bottom of Mom's closet.

In and out of court we went as they fought their way through the aftermath of divorce. The dysfunction and strife continued, and I struggled to find balance between the two of them.

Wounded and feeling the only way to heal was to somehow get her attention, to make her love me the way she loved my brothers and even my cousin, I spent days driving to Northern Montana where she now called home. I drove through the night. I was exhausted after school, training, and work driving through blizzards of snow. Pappa begged me not to go and became increasingly frustrated that I spent so much time seeking her approval.

The night began innocently enough. A Friday night, tension due to the divorce and constant battles was present, but I did not recognize how present. Pappa and Sinda went out drinking to let off steam. Linda and I stayed home, listening to music and tormenting each other.

My head just sank into my pillow preparing for sleep when a crash came from the front door, shouting, hurried footsteps, and screams. Jumping from bed and bursting into the hall, I could hear Sinda's voice tore through the house, "Louis, NO!"

Pushing my way into the bedroom every hair on my neck standing on end, I saw Pappa loading a rifle.

LIFTED UP

"I've had it! I'm going to kill that Bitch!" Bullets dropping into the barrel and more into his pockets.

Darkness dropped through my mind. Mom had just had my sister, and she would be home with her. I could not stomach the thought of that baby lying there next to her dead mother.

Instinctively and unabashedly, I stepped in front of Pappa, planted my feet, and declared that I was not going to allow him to leave. As if I could stop this storm of a man even on a calm day.

A 4-poster queen bed stood in the middle of the room. Pappa and I on one side facing off in the narrow path between the bed and the wall.

"Move!" he shouted. "I'm going to kill her and stop this madness!"

Sinda's shrill screaming was still cutting through the room from the other corner. I refused to move. Eye to eye we met. As quickly as lightning follows thunder on a hot summer's day, his hand came smashing across me. Like a rag doll, I flung across the bed, feet flying in the air, body crashing into the wall on the other side.

He had never struck me like that before! What the hell just happened? Before I could get my senses, my pride, and my jaw off the floor, he was gone, rifle and all.

Panicked and pissed off without reasoning, I grasped for a few belongings and my wallet. I had enough of this madness. I was running away from this craziness! Where to? Who the hell cared!

Sinda's voice was now replaced with Linda's. Terrified and begging me not to go, she clung to me.

In the moment, it never dawned on me how terrified she was. She would be all-alone, our parents were gone, and who knew if they would live the night.

None of that even crossed my mind, as I kicked her off me. I no longer gave a shit about anything.

Darkness! Northern Idaho chill air and a black sky dotted with stars greeted me as I stormed out of the door on my way to an undetermined destination.

Anger flooded my veins as my feet stomped the blacktop. Surrounded by darkness and pine trees, I marched down the road toward town. One by one, lengthy intervals between cars passed by. Gathering my thoughts, a bit, I decide to hitch hike. I just wanted to get as far away as I could.

Damn it! A police car. The officer pulled up next to me, commanding me to get in the car. I tried to refuse, but in the end could not disobey. I refused to let him take me home. Crying and growling in anger, I let him know I would never go back there.

I spent that night at a safe house. All the windows blocked, people posted at the doors, and eyes on me all night. In the light of day when all had been cleared, I was sent back to the custody of my Pappa.

He could not even look at me, he was still so furious at me. He could not begin to understand how I could stand up for her after all she had done to me. After all she had done to us!

Within a few months, I packed and moved to Montana to live with Mom. Life at home had become so volatile. There was drinking and fighting between Pappa and Sinda. I was still mad, he was still mad, and our magic connection had tattered.

Pappa's once comforting voice damned me and warned me not to leave or never come back. Stoic, I climbed into my packed car and drove down the long drive to the highway.

LIFTED UP

Only when my car was out of sight of Pappa did I cry. Once the tears started, I think they continued the entire drive to Montana, and Libby, my new home.

"Walk with me, Daddy.
Walk alongside me, Daddy and hold my little hand. I have so many things to learn that I don't yet understand.
Teach me things to keep me safe from dangers every day. Show me how to do my best at home, at school, at play. Every child needs a gentle hand to guide them as they grow. So walk alongside me, Daddy.
We have a long way to go."
Helen Bush

CHAPTER 8

WILD WEST IN LOGGER TOWN

"But the West of the old times, with its strong characters, its stern battles, its tremendous stretches of loneliness can never be blotted from my mind."
Buffalo Bill

Still wanting her love so much, I arrived in Libby. That day I finally made some headway. There was love in her eyes as I stepped into the house and even a hug.

My baby sister squealed, and I scooped her up holding her tight, so happy she had not suffered some unspeakable fate.

Transition into this school was easier. Still an introvert and an oddball, I did not quite fit in.

Religion was still huge for me. My Bible and my God were what seemed to hold me together through all that had transpired over the past few years. The Church of the Nazarene was where we attended. I was at church 5 days a week for activities, Bible study, youth group, and church services.

The trick was, when not at church, I hung out with my friend from Bonners in her apartment downtown. Drinking, boys, and music filled

LIFTED UP

our time together. Rebellion had begun to settle in, and I took it out on the boys who crossed our path. It did not last long. Tammi's family finally insisted she move back to Bonners Ferry.

I had begun living a life of duality inside and out. Really, I had been living that life for many years now. Soul fractured and searching for ground, I stood with one foot in each world.

Sitting on the edge of the desktop, Bible perched in my hands, I stared back at the two debating with me. Lunchtimes were spent sitting in a classroom battling over which religion was more right—traditional Christianity, Jehovah's Witness, or Latter-Day Saints.

I still did not feel like I fit in anywhere, so I began to claim the "weirdness" that was me.

"'Cause I'm back
Yes, I'm back
Well, I'm back
Yes, I'm back
Well, I'm back, back
Well, I'm back in black
Yes, I'm back in black"
AC/DC

I dyed my hair every so often, showing up at school with red hair, sometimes blond hair, and even black hair. Walking into school one day with freshly dyed black hair, one of the wrestlers whom I had a huge crush on started singing AC/DC's *Back in Black* as soon as he saw me step through the door. It became my call song for months afterward.

Little round face beaming up at me, mornings meant getting baby sister up and ready for the day. Mornings meant singing, "You are my sunshine" to her as she clung cheerfully to the edge of her crib. Eventually she would sing it upon waking as her alarm that she was now awake!

Adoring her does not even begin to describe how I felt about her. I loved babies, and this one was my wee sister. Taking care of her was a joy and release for me.

But taking care of her began taking over my teenage life. I got her up and fed her in the mornings, put her to bed at night, and was required to take her with me wherever I went if it was not school or work.

Basketball games, football games, outings with friends, or country bike rides all meant packing her along with me. I really did not mind. I loved her so much!

I was the new kid at school, and toting a baby with me everywhere I went, the rumors began to fly. The perception and word were that she was my child. To further that illusion, she had begun to mistakenly call me "Mom" because I had become her primary caregiver.

Mom and I had multiple fights over this. I grew a pair and told her that if it continued, I would have to be allowed to adopt her as she did not know whom her mother was! It took some time but reprogramming the duties and her perception began and slowly took hold, releasing me from the "mom" spot in her life.

Trading that duty meant workload shifted, and soon I was working in the western wear shop my stepdad owned with his uncle and cousin. I was not paid. I was just required to work. It was more than confusing because my brothers were not required to work in the shop and were allowed time and freedom to have personal lives, but not me. Resentment began to grow roots in my subconscious, along with the continuation of the message that I was not enough. Wanting some distance and a chance to get out a little, I took a job in a nursing home as a nurse's aide. I spent weekends working the early morning shift there, requiring me to leave home by 5:30 am on Saturday and Sunday.

My younger brother and I shared a vehicle. It was meant for work and for trips to youth group. He had begun dating the pastor's daughter, and they planned a trip to Kalispell, which was over an hour away. Their date night came and off they went.

He arrived home somewhere after midnight, and I could finally sleep knowing that the vehicle would be there, so I could go to work. Up at 4:30 am and preparing for work, I was still tired from waiting up the night before. The air was crisp and cold as I carried my lunch out to the car to warm it up for the trip to work.

The engine groaned and strained, started and stalled, several times before settling in and running. The gas gauge caught my sleepy eyes, and I realized the car I had left with a full tank was on empty. We lived in the country several miles out of town. There was not enough gas to get me to town and no gas station nearby to fill the tank up.

I needed to get to work! How? Remembering that my stepdad had a 50-gallon gas tank he kept fuel in for his used auto lot nestled on the highway, I decided to ask if I could get enough gas to get to town.

I went back up the stairs and into the house. Everyone was asleep. Knocking on their door, I sheepishly asked to "borrow" enough gas to get to town. Mom and my stepdad were both irritated and angry. Mom started yelling at me for being so irresponsible, and my stepdad went to put gas in the car without saying too much.

Frustrated, I barked back at Mom about how I did not leave the tank empty. It had come back empty from my brother's date the night before after midnight. Oh yeah, and by the way, how is it he gets to stay out so late and I have to be in by 10 pm, IF I got to go out at all?

That was it. I was now firmly in trouble.

Grounded, I could not drive or use any of the vehicles. I had to take the bus to school and ride my bike to town to get to work. I pleaded, reiterating that I had not been at fault. It did not matter that my younger brother had been the cause of the problem, I was the one grounded. He continued using the car at will.

There it was—another brick in the wall. I felt so useless. I felt that no matter what I did or how good I was, I would be punished. It was not the only time that I was punished for something my brothers did, and it certainly would not be the last.

Questioning my move to Montana, my heart missed Pappa so. I had written him several letters. I was not allowed to use the phone to call him, so writing was all I could manage.

One cloudy afternoon, depression looming, I arrived at home from school and went to my room to ponder where my Pappa was and why he did not write me. Quietly, I lay on the bed and cried.

After about 20 minutes, the door flung open to the darkened room and light came blinding in from the chandelier in the dining room. Mom's silhouette framed in the harsh light. Holding back the tears as best I could, I turned to look and see what she wanted. A flutter of white envelopes came flying at me. All the letters I wrote Pappa had been returned, and she had been holding onto them.

Disbelief shook me as I tried to comprehend the loss of contact with my hero and my savior. What had I done? Why did I ever move here and leave him?

Maniacal laughing began rumbling up from her, "You will never see him again! He moved and did not even tell you! He's gone! Even he does not love you!"

LIFTED UP

Panic began to sink in, and tears turned to heaving as I struggled to hold back the need to vomit.

Slam! The door shook my room as she took her exit. Still laughing on the other side of the door taunting me about how stupid and worthless I was and how I would never see him. She taunted if even he did not want me, no one ever would.

Bricks upon bricks cemented onto that subconscious wall of never enough, unloved, unwanted, and unseen. Cracks covered the landscape of my heart.

I spent that night in my room with my head spinning and heart breaking.

Outwardly, the Montana world did not see the pain that was my life. I smiled, played, and laughed with friends and youth group when I wasn't at home.

Little did I know, Mom had begun to build a story of how emotionally and mentally unstable I was. The adults, and even some of my older friends, didn't tell me about the picture she was painting. The story had been crafted. Church members prayed for my sanity, for my purity, and for my soul based on the stories she imparted to the congregation. Things at home became increasingly difficult. I was punished more and more for my brothers' actions. My old friend, the ulcer, had returned. I could not eat without pain. Vomiting after

MISHA FAYANT

eating was a regular occurrence that eventually began producing blood again.

Knowing that I did not have Pappa to run to when I needed him, things became darker for me day by day. Verbal assaults and more instances loomed over me assuring me that I meant nothing to anyone, that I was unwanted, fat, unattractive, stupid, and because of my recent promiscuity, unclean even to God.

I had not been allowed to check the mail for months. Somehow, I snuck down and began checking the mail when I thought she would be unaware. Finally, a letter from Pappa. It turns out he had written me and had tried to notify me of the move, but she had stolen the letters. They weren't the only letters stolen. Letters from friends back in Idaho were stolen and read. Some made it to me, but most did not.

Spring came and with it track and field season! Finally, I enrolled in the team and began practicing the throwing events that I loved—shotput and discus.

There was always a ton of horseplay going on during our mostly unsupervised practices. One of the older boys and I had been play fighting. He was cocky, and I was not backing down.

I felt his grip on my wrist as my arm violently twisted behind my back, and searing pain shot down my shoulder. I let out a scream, and I crumbled to the ground. My shoulder had been dislocated.

Cold grass pressing against my face, tears of pain running from my eyes, I laid in the grass, took a deep breath and pressed my shoulder to the ground trying to push it back into place.

This older boy thought I was faking it. Catcalls came hurling my way, goading me. I was so furious and in so much pain, I ignored his voice and focused on fixing my shoulder.

Just as I felt the shoulder pop back into place, I heard a thud then felt crushing pressure on the back of my head, just as his voice rang

LIFTED UP

out, "Heads up!"He had tossed that 12-pound shot put, intending to hit close to me and scare me. Instead, the heavy metal ball hit the back of my head leaving an indentation in the skull and pushing my face into the ground.

Footsteps rushed toward me. Voices yelled, "Are you okay?" Hands grabbed my arms and turned me over. They sat me upright. Eyes staring into mine.

Bob, my younger brother, was a runner. Someone had informed him of what happened, and in the blink of an eye, he was there to help.

Agitated, I wanted to be left alone. I was fine. I just wanted to practice!

I swore I walked to the car that took me to the hospital. My brother later told me, "Your legs were moving, but they weren't holding you. We carried you out!"

I had a concussion! A head injury that would be the excuse for being called mentally unstable well into my adulthood.

My psyche continued to be damaged, not only was every incident used against me and my mental state, control that toyed with my mental stability seeped into every corner of my life.

When I first moved to Montana with her, I would check the mail and to my surprise hardcore pornography filled the mailbox. Gay pornography, images I was curious about and did not understand. The men who had lived there before she married my stepdad had an incestual gay relationship and the remnants of it flooded the mail.

That was the beginning of not being able to check the mail. I found it humorous and educating. There was a lot of explaining to be done in this Western mountain town. That, of course, frustrated Mom, but eventually I was told the details of the relationship and the men who had inhabited the house in the past.

MISHA FAYANT

Cloyd had been the founder of the western wear shop and housed his nephew with whom he had a sexual relationship. Cloyd had passed away and the nephew had moved on to a bigger city, somewhere where his lifestyle could be accommodated.

There were other stories, so many stories, of sex and cheating. I remember one woman in town she was jealous of because my stepdad had dated her before Mom. Her favorite joke was to call the woman "Porcupine" because that's what she would look like if she had as many sticking out of her as she had stuck in her. It was said so matter of fact. I wanted to be accepted by Mom, so I laughed and joined in with the jokes.

The odd thing was, there were times when I almost felt like I could be accepted, and all would be okay. We shared stories, shared time, and had laughs. There were even times that I spent on the couch with her holding my head, stroking my hair. I felt hope in those moments.

Then without warning, the shadow side would return. It was not just that I understood her actions in a certain way; it was the direct language she used. Time and again, it was a message of not being enough, not pretty enough, not smart enough, not talented enough, not thin enough— just never enough.

I felt like a prisoner of war. I was convinced that I did not matter to her, only the fact that she had won, and Dad had lost by me not being with him.

Ulcer worsening, tension in the house growing, I knew I could not take much more. I was able to contact Pappa through letters once I had his new address.

I made the trip to Washington to visit him where he was living. The day seemed so bright, and I felt so much joy. I had not told Mom the reality of why I was going. I was sent to pick up parts and supplies for the small shop in Montana. I took the opportunity to seek out and visit Pappa without her knowing.

The house he lived in was on a street lined with trees and older homes. The neighborhood was a little sketchy, and most of the people on the street lived in poverty. Car break-ins were common.

Anticipation building, I stood on the porch of the little white house with blue trim knocking on the door. Sinda, my stepmom, answered the door. My eyes darted, searching for Pappa. "He's over there on the couch," she pointed to a brown leather couch backed up against the living room wall.

Lying on the couch, covered in blankets, his eyes opened and looked to me. His blue eyes that I loved so much were replaced with a cloudy grey. His voice trembled softly, and I had to strain to hear him.

Confused, my gaze sought out Sinda, questioning what was happening. Pappa was the most vibrant man I had ever known. Why was he so pale and unable to get up?

"I'm falling apart
I'm barely breathing
With a broken heart
That's still beating."
Lifehouse

"The doctors cannot figure out what's wrong with him. One doctor said he is dying of a broken heart." She informed me.

Rushing to his side, I crouched on the floor next to him and touched his cheek. This was my fault! I had left him and broke his heart! How could I ever forgive myself if he died!? I spent the afternoon holding his head, stroking his hair, and apologizing, telling him how much I loved and needed him.

We devised a plan of how to communicate and how to make a plan for me to move back to be with him. It took a few months, but his health began to improve. Soon he was himself again.

He found a cabin on a small lake in the woods outside of a small Washington border town—a place where he could heal and reconnect with the earth and his heritage.

Returning to Montana, I had to pretend that nothing was amiss. Planning my escape, we set a date and time.

Quietly and carefully, I began to gather and pack my belongings in a way that I hoped would not be noticed. My nerves were on overdrive terrified of the wrath if it was found out I was planning to leave.

I knew that if I told Mom, I would not be allowed to leave, and I would truly be a prisoner. It had to be done in secret.

The day finally arrived. Mom was gone. No one was home. I loaded my car and drove into town to the parking lot where Pappa agreed to meet me. We moved everything into his car, and we were ready to go!

One last thing I had been putting money away in an account at the local bank. I asked Pappa if we could stop and retrieve the money, and he cautiously agreed.

Pappa at the wheel, we pulled into the bank drive thru to retrieve my funds. The woman helping us at the bank was someone I knew from our church. There was a look of concern on her face, but I thought nothing of it. She explained that it would take a minute to get everything in order.

Pappa and I sat in that truck laughing and telling stories, so happy to be together once again. It seemed to be taking a long time! What was the issue? He buzzed the teller. Her face showing signs of confusion and nerves, she told him it would only be a few minutes longer.

Our conversation continued, and we were so lost in reconnecting that we did not notice the vehicles suddenly surrounding us.

Laughter and agitation at having to wait so long filled the truck cab. Suddenly, loud voices, yelling, and tires screeching interrupted our fun. Looking out the windows, we were faced with a barricade of police cars surrounding us, and officers standing offensively, weapons drawn. Revolvers, rifles, and even a shotgun or two were aimed at us!

I looked around to see if one of the other cars was trying to rob the bank! Nope! All this attention was directed at Pappa and me. There was more screaming and commands to get out of the car. We were forced to the ground, faces in the pavement, and hands pulled behind our backs.

Mom had told such a good story of my psychological breakdown and Pappa's abusive history that we were treated like Bonnie and Clyde.

Hauled off to the police station, I frantically tried to explain that he was my Dad! There was joint custody! I was 15 and had a right to be in his custody per the Idaho courts.

Those Montana lawmen were having none of it. He was interrogated and forced to leave. Threats ensued. He was told he was not allowed back into town ever or jail would be the least of his worries.

I was forced to be held in a cell until Mom found time to come retrieve me. I begged. I pleaded. I told stories of fear. I spoke of the law and

my right to be in Dad's custody. None of it mattered. This was their town, and they would decide what happened here.

I spent hours begging them not to make me go back home, telling them I did not feel safe. Nothing worked. I was forced back into her custody.

The situation at home worsened. I was watched constantly and restricted. If I was not working at the retirement home, I was expected to work at the shop.

Once again, I began to devise a plan. It took some time, but my belongings were again prepped for a speedy retreat.

Blood hitting the toilet as I kneeled over the porcelain became a daily occurrence. Friends began to worry. I was losing weight. My face was thin, pale, and drawn. Tremors kept my hands from being steady. Sleep was impossible.

Finally! The family planned a trip to cut firewood, I was expected to go and told I would not be allowed to stay home. The morning came, and I got up early forcing myself to throw up. Guttural sounds filled the house all morning. I spiked a fever (fear fever). My stepdad instructed Mom to let me stay home.

I waited 20 minutes after they left, huddled under my blankets trembling with anxiety. As quickly as I could, I once again placed my belongings in the vehicle. I did not want to leave the home unlocked and be responsible for vandalism. I locked all the doors and crawled out a second story window, leaving the key on my nightstand.

Fifteen minutes felt like fifteen hours as I drove to the opposite side of

LIFTED UP

town and across the county line to where I met Pappa. Neither one of us seemed to take a breath until we reached the Idaho line. Squeals of victory rang out as we crossed the Idaho line! I was back with Dad where I belonged, and no one could force me back now.

"The secret to happiness is freedom . . .
And the secret to freedom is courage."
Thucydides

CHAPTER 9

SENIOR YEAR AND CANADA

*"If we were meant to stay in one place,
we'd have roots instead of feet . . ."*
Rachel Wolchin

The stately log cabin was perched on a hill overlooking a man-made lake, tucked into the mountain woods. As we drove up the winding backcountry road, I began to wonder if we would ever arrive. Just when I thought we would be lost forever deep in the woods, there it was. My heart stopped. It was so serene and beautiful.

My lungs filled with the fresh cool air as I drank in the freedom and comfort of being back with Pappa. This home was a perfect place for us. Hidden away, he chose it knowing Mom would not find us here.

The cabin had been built to be a resort lodge, but the builder abandoned plans for the surrounding cabins and so it stood a lone sentinel watching over the lake and wildlife that filled the trees and water.

My smile came back, my heart lightened, and there was an odd sense of peace that wrapped around me. Ducks, chickens, and dogs ran the grassy knoll behind the house. Fish jumped when ducks

LIFTED UP

dove in pursuit across the lake. Deer and rabbits bounded through the woods surrounding us. It was heaven on earth.

"Everything in the forest has its season.
Where one thing falls, another grows.
Maybe not what was there before,
but something new and wonderful all the same."
Bambi 2

Walking quietly through the woods, Pappa showed me how to quiet the soul and "talk" with the animals. They would just come up to him without fear, eat from his hand, nuzzle him, and run around his feet. It was like watching a Native Merlin weave his magic.

I had one last school to enroll in, and it was brand new. In fact, they were still finishing the building when we started school in the fall. It was my senior year, and I was plunked in the middle of strangers, but it was exciting.

This time I made friends easier than in the past. Social activities filled my time. The challenge was that we lived so far out of town. We did not have much money so use of the car was limited to necessities. That year, I rode my bike more than ever. It was 10 miles to town.

Spring came and with it track season. Track practice meant I could not get home by bus. The only answer was to ride my bike. Every morning, I rode out in the cold mist, backpack strapped on, and rode into town in time to clean up, change, and be ready for my first class of the day. Afternoons meant practice. After I would make the trip home. Sometimes, I was so tired my legs already felt like rubber. Riding home was uphill all the way. I would get tired, but I would fight to beat the darkness that would be looming and chasing me the whole way. I loved those rides. They made me feel like a warrior.

All too soon the end of the year neared. My friends had graduation parties planned. We did not have enough money to do anything but get my cap and gown. It was okay with me. I had a good year and that was reward enough!

My heart never let go of Mom. Though there were some battles left, I loved her and had tried to repair what I could of our relationship. I sent her a graduation invitation, but as expected she did not come. Pappa was there though! Beaming proud and blues eyes sparkling, he stood tall. I graduated in the top 10% of my class.

That night, I was invited to my best friend's graduation party. It was quite the event with tons of family and friends and even more presents. I was just happy to be there for her and to be included! Later her mother hugged me, tears in her eyes, and said something about how gracious and unselfish I was, never once asking for attention to be drawn from her daughter, even though I had nothing. I was shocked. What else would I do? She was my friend and had supported me in this new place all year long.

It was now time for Canada and my post-graduation adventure. Candy was a rebellious friend of ours. She was a spitfire! She had plans to move to Canada where her grandparents lived. She wanted freedom from the small town and the control of her parents who were business owners in town. She asked me to go along with her, and there I felt no hesitation when I agreed with Pappa's blessing.

Our tribe was historically nomadic, moving between Canada and the US. I had until I was 21 to declare where I would be a permanent resident, so I went to Canada to find escape. It felt like I was moving across the ocean to a foreign country.

Music blaring and the windows wide open, we each drove our cars north toward the unknown. Van Halen, REO Speedwagon, Air Supply,

LIFTED UP

and Hall and Oates fueled our mood and escape. Summer sun graced our drive. Passing construction workers, we would taunt them as young girls do. We found it hilarious and exhilarating.

Trail, BC was tucked in the valley between steep hillsides. The route in and out of town meant steep grade roads that required caution. Houses and business seemed built into the rock hillsides. Narrow streets and narrow, tall houses filled the hills rising out of the valley.

Canada-ese was a whole new language for me. Words had a totally different meaning than they did stateside. Simple words like "pissed" did not mean angry. It meant "piss drunk".

Hockey, kickboxing, sex, and getting "pissed" were the past times in Trail. Athletic, unabashed men, band members, summer sun, and wild nights—we explored almost all that was offered to us. I was even introduced to the strip club and half naked women dancing in ways I had never seen.

We were two young American girls North of the border, running rampant in town drinking, partying, and expanding our social circle. It all seemed fun, but that was about to change.

Between appeals to the government to establish residency, we searched for jobs.

One afternoon donning form fitting dresses and stiletto heels, we strolled into a historic and posh hotel looking for work.

Striped suit, white shirt, and a dark tie, he sat in the center of the room smoking a cigar and watching our every move. Soon another dark suited man was sent to retrieve us. His voice was as smooth as his manners as he struck up conversation with us, prying so stealthily that neither of us understood what was really happening.

He made us an offer to work for him. How exciting! We gathered his name, as he did ours, before we were excused. Arriving at her grandparents' house, we excitedly told them of the handsome, suave man who was going to hire us. Caution struck their faces as they asked if we knew his name and where we found him. Giving them the required information, they told us he was none other than the local mafia leader and pimp. Working for him would mean no innocent business.

My heart sank, and goosebumps ran up my spine. How could this be? He was so nice! Needless to say, we avoided further contact with him. But that would not be the end of it. Soon I realized that I was constantly being followed and watched. Dark cars that were not recognized by the neighbors parked down the street every night. Watching. Waiting. It was nerve wracking!

My car's alternator was starting to go out. Often it would not start right away, and I would have to fiddle with it to get it running. It was annoying!

I continued to search for employment. Smack in the middle of downtown and just down the street from that fateful hotel was a Chinese restaurant. I was called for an interview, but it meant I had to arrive in the evening after dark. I parked around the corner down the street, as there was no parking close to the front door that night.

"A mob is not, as is so often said, mindless.
A mob is single-minded."
Teju Col

The walk to the interview was uneventful. No one seemed to even notice that I was there. Thank goodness! It had been an unexpectedly busy night at the restaurant, and time drug by waiting for the owner to break away and come talk to me. Finally, we were able to speak. They made me an offer to start work, but I would need to provide them some specific documentation. Yes! A job!

Relief and excitement carried me out the door into the dark, cool night. Wrapping my jacket around to chase away the chill, I noticed a dark suit across the street watching me. The door to the restaurant was already locked. Feet don't fail me now! It felt as if every hair on my body stood on end as I hurried down the street toward my car, trying not to draw too much attention. Maybe I was wrong about the suit.

*"I'm trying to keep a level head.
You have to be careful out in the world.
It's so easy to get turned."*
Elvis Presley

Looking over my shoulder, he had crossed the street and was following me. My eyes darting forward, the sight of a second suit coming up the street eyes fixated on me came into view. Out of nowhere, a third dark suit appeared. Now, the kind of horror that you feel when in a dream unable to scream tormented me. I made it to the car and clamored in as quickly as I could. Fumbling, my keys missed their target. One more try, and a quick turn to the right. Nothing but a slow groan. Oh, please! Please just start! Another try. Another groan. They were closing in. Please, damn it start! One last try, and the engine fired, gears ground, and tires squealed as the car roared away nearly running one of the men down.

MISHA FAYANT

I went straight home. No drinking. No parties. Just home!

Friends from town warned that he was intent on taking me. The suits would not move if there were others around. They were waiting for the opportunity to find me alone.

I was told stories of what would happen to me. Stories of "favored" girls of the past and the tasks they had to perform came trickling in. At first, I was naïve enough to believe it could not happen to me. More incidents and all too close calls, and there was no denying that I was not safe.

Without a word to anyone, my things were packed. Early one morning while the household slept, I checked the road for the dark cars that had waited for months. It was clear. They had gone. Quietly, my bags were tucked into the car with as little disruption as I could muster, and I drove away from that little home on the hill.

Stomach churning and my nerves on high alert, my car and I slithered through town in the quiet of the morning. Finally, at the east edge of town topping the hill, I took a breath filling my lungs and sped down the almost deserted highway toward the border.

LIFTED UP

CHAPTER 10

A BROKEN PATH

*"Family is supposed to be our safe haven. Very often,
it's the place where we find the deepest heartache."*
Iyanla Vanzant

I made a promise to stop and visit my younger sister in Montana before leaving that morning. Back to Montana I went with every hope in my heart of repairing things with Mom and my brothers. I missed my family.

Bright blue skies escorted me on the long drive across the Crowsnest Highway. Quiet mountain beauty was all that surrounded me. After all the commotion of the summer in Trail and that close call I narrowly escaped, it was a welcome drive. I had time to breathe, relax, and reflect before arriving in Montana.

Eyes weary from the 4-hour drive in blinding sun, I finally pulled up to the barn red two-story structure that held both Mom's store and the living quarters above. My heart raced as I climbed the stairs that scaled the southside of the structure. What would it be like this time?

As I entered the living quarters, I found my older brother, Louis, lying on the couch. Unbeknownst to me, he had come home from college for a visit. Cold daggers shot at me as I stepped into the

LIFTED UP

living room. He did not feign politeness or pretend that he liked or cared for me in any way. Quivering, I managed a smile and asked how he was—no reply. Branding irons landed over and over on the surface of my heart. We once had a family that may have been dysfunctional, but I thought we loved each other!

My older brother hated me. I know this because he told me repeatedly, spit on me, and made constant threats.

Eyes of fire stared me down; his stout 6' body loomed at me menacingly, as his deep booming voice shouted. The year before when I made my escape, he said Mom had a nervous breakdown. Reports came slamming at me that she broke down, incapable of functioning. Tears and wailing filled the house. It was all my fault for leaving!

Seething anger built in my bones as he flung vile words my way. Blaming, shaming, accusations of selfishness, and there it was— "Bitch!" In my mind, the only reason she would breakdown was facing the reality that she had lost. I did not believe that I mattered to her as much as her ownership of me, a symbol of triumphing over Pappa. I knew or believed somewhere inside that she loved me. I also believed that my wellbeing, my whereabouts bore little consequence for her conscience beyond the battle between her and Pappa. From my point of view, I was nothing but a pawn, one that could be set aside and shelved all too easily when not in use.

While in Canada, I had asked a friend to make cassette tapes of some amazing Canadian bands for me, and I invested in several others. I was excited to share the good points of my adventure and shared the sounds of these bands with my sister. Louis pretended not to pay attention to me, but little did I know he was plotting the seeds of his revenge for me hurting Mom the whole time.

That summer I met a young French boy who was visiting as a summer exchange student. I knew a little French (un pettit peu). His host family had asked if I would be his companion and guide for the short time he had left in Montana. Excited by another adventure, I agreed to meet him. Fabrice Phillipe Giuliano was so handsome with dark thick hair and even darker eyes. There was an instant spark. I agreed!

"In every girl's life, there is a boy she will
never forget and a summer where it all began."
Lifehouse

He was artistic. His thick smooth French accent was mesmerizing. I could not get enough of him. He was a drummer and a talented musician. Motley Crue, a band I had never heard of, was his American obsession. I have always loved music. It feeds my soul. He seemed so perfect for me—God sent.

Our days were spent exploring the evergreen forests, the reservoir behind the dam, parks, and attending events. Mostly we sought out the solace of the forests where we spent our days curled up in the back of my little old station wagon. I learned French. He learned English. My heart expanded and felt full. No one else mattered to us as we spent those hot dry days hiding in the woods, keeping our love from everyone else. Days and days spent loving and making love in the hot summer sun.

Interrupted! Mom had caught on to our relationship. How could anyone not? I was beaming, singing French songs, I could not stop smiling, and my soul shone like a diamond. He only had one week left before departing for home in the suburbs of Paris.

Mom commanded that I go on a trip with her to pick up a car that my stepdad had purchased for his lot. What the hell! I may as well go. Maybe this was an olive branch. Perhaps she needed me and wanted to spend time with me, so on the trip we went. I soon I forgot about my brother as Mom and I chattered and laughed cruising in the Montana sun.

A few days passed before we returned home. Louis had left for North Idaho College soon after we departed on the trip. Ready for some alone time with my music, I headed to where my bags had been left. In the dark and cool open area at the back of the home, I planned to lie down, put my earphones in, and listen to the music from Canada that I had grown to love.

Gone! It was all gone! Without hesitation I knew that Louis had taken my music along with a few other personal items. Fury! I was so completely over his narcissistic, no one else matters, bullying bullshit!

Fabrice and I were no longer afforded time together when I returned. We had to make covert plans to meet on the back roads between our houses. We were in love, and Mom did all she could to rip his presence from me. I could not understand why!

In my mind, it made her horribly hypocritical to judge me for sharing myself with a boy I loved so very much, when she had multiple affairs while married to Pappa.

All the joy and peace that had been found in the last month was swept away with hurricane force. Saying goodbye to Fabrice shredded my heart. Anger built at the realization that our time together had been impeded. Why must I always be tormented?

As soon as he left, I packed my wagon and headed back to Idaho. Another opportunity to heal wounds only ended in creating more. The old wounds deepened, and my self-worth eroded just a little further.

Pappa had moved from Washington to a nearby North Idaho town. Back in the limits of a city, we lived in a small two-story home with a huge yard and detached garage.

MISHA FAYANT

He was rebuilding his income for the umpteenth time. Working as a mechanic and striving to start his own small business logging post and poles, money was tight.

He had been rebuilding an old Ford ¾ ton pickup into a full-size logging truck. Pappa was so creative, innovative, and driven. It could pull a trailer built for hauling post and poles. When not out in the woods, he was home doing what he loved best. Creating!

Slowly he hired crews to come work with him. I wanted to be a part of whatever he did. I begged and begged to be allowed to work on his "crew". Finally, one day he was shorthanded, and I was allowed to go out with him.

I was elated to swing a hatchet, knock back limbs, and clean the timber in the hot, dry dusty woods! I got to go out and be with Pappa.

At the end of the day, grasping the truck handle, pain searing my swollen forearms, I could not pull it to open it. The day had gone fast, even in the summer heat. I pushed through, determined to make Pappa proud and show him I could do it.

His crooked smile found me from across the truck cab, "What's the matter, my girl? Can't open the door?" he asked letting out a small knowing chuckle. Laughter between complaints of "Holy crap, they hurt!" filled the cab the entire ride home.

Time passed, and I proved myself daily, earning more duties and learning more skills every day. I eventually was tasked with running the heavy equipment which ranged from a dozer to a skidder to the truck and self-loader.

Hanging on for dear life, I clung to the controls of the skidder as it began tipping up onto the driver's side tires. Towing a load of fresh fallen trees, my first go at operating the skidder was turning into a battle. Navigation from the fell area to the deck required some tricky maneuvers, which Pappa and I did not agree on. Screaming at each other, we fought over which course to take. I have always been extremely good at fitting pieces together and seeing the path. I wanted to turn right. He wanted me to turn left. I told him it would not work. He growled and told me to do what he said. Angrily, I followed his direction and now everything I feared would occur was happening. The load was binding, causing the skidder to turn on its side. Dangling from the cab, it was a close call. I let go of the controls in time to keep us from tipping over. It did not happen often, but I was right!

A huge belly laugh exploded from Pappa as all 4 wheels touched the ground again. He was laughing because his girl was so smart. These are the things I lived for with him. His sense of pride in me kept me sane and kept the looming depression from taking me over completely.

Operating a caterpillar was next on the agenda, and finally, the truck and loader. Eventually, it became my job to load, haul, and unload the cargo at the mill.

That summer was fraught with injury for me adding to the toll of my broken bones.

One hot summer day, Pappa and the only crew member left that day had gone to town for something, leaving me at the deck cleaning, chain saw in hand. There was so much to do before they returned. The Australian band Men at Work blared in my headphones as I worked through focused on having as much done as I could before they returned.

I ignored the intense heat, attributing it to dry summer heat and hard work. Soon, there was a thick smoke I could not ignore. Forest fire! I was caught right in the middle. The fire had swept through, blocking me from the equipment, which now seemed so far away. (Again, there were no cell phones, and I had no way to notify anyone).

Pappa, my hero, arrived in time to hop on the Cat and doze an earthen path out of the fire. He saved my life that day. It was horrifying in the moment. We laughed about Fayant luck and cheating death while driving home after fighting the fire and winning. Pappa told more stories of some of the multiple times he had cheated death as we drove.

Attached to the back of the cab, the self-loader consisted of a seat, controls, a large folding boom arm, and on the end a "clam" that opened and closed picking up the logs and depositing them on the back of the truck. The equipment takes quite a toll out there in the wilderness, and the clam had broken.

It lay in the shop at home waiting for parts and Pappa's touch to fix it. In its place was a simple metal cable called a choker. This meant I had to get down every "pick" of the posts to wrap the choker, climb up, use the controls to lift the load, and then climb onto the truck bed to unhook and adjust the load.

Crawling into the perch of a seat became an extra step that took too much time and energy, so I stood behind the cab and operated the controls. Maneuvering one load onto the deck, I heard a snap and a loud "swoosh", accompanied by a spurting black fountain.

It all happened so fast. The load came crashing back at me as the hydraulic hose failed. A deafening shriek emitted from my lungs as those logs crushed my ankle, pinning me to the cab.

My ankle bound and swollen, Pappa would not let me return to the woods until the swelling was down. I wanted so much to prove to him that I was worthy. I begged to go even though I could barely walk.

Tiring of my insistence, he finally let me return. The injuries began again—a hand, a forearm, and finally a concussion.

Money was tight. The clam never got fixed to keep me from climbing up and down on the truck. My ankle still injured, I stayed on the ground hooking the choker.

LIFTED UP

The truck bed had metal uprights to hold the logs. Those uprights had extensions placed in once the load reached high enough to allow for more logs to be placed on the truck.

The extensions were not yet in. Pappa was up on the load rolling post logs into place to even the load. I was on the ground hooking the choker. Bent over feeding the choker around the next load, I heard a boot slip, followed by, "Oh shit! Look out!" Before I could move, a series of poles came rolling off the deck of the truck, landing one at a time on the back of my head, pounding me into the dirt face first and knocking me unconscious.

Coming to, Pappa plucked me from the earth and propped me up. Stars swirling, head aching, and throbbing, I struggled to focus. My eyes began to clear, my hand on the back of my head, all I could see were big blue eyes looking back at me drowned in tears.

That day, he refused to allow me back in the woods ever again. What had been a joke was now all too painfully real that he could lose his girl.

Frustration ran through me as I pleaded to be allowed to continue working with him, but his refusal was final. I never got to go back out with him.

During those days working in the woods, I had a thirst for life. I wanted to make the most of every moment I had.

Dirty, dusty, flannel wearing 19-year-old by day, I cleaned up pretty well by afternoon. Even as a young girl, I felt this urgency in life to do as much as I could. Life seemed to be going by so fast, and I did not want to waste a minute of it.

I made the trek to town on weekends. Dressed in form fitting "girl" clothes, I spent the evenings in the local dance clubs until the early hours of the morning.

MISHA FAYANT

One Saturday evening, I ran into my older brother at one of the dance clubs. Thankfully, friends kept us separated. Drinks made me numb to his presence and allowed me to focus on my friend's laughter. Drinking and driving is never a good idea, but it's something I did most every weekend. That weekend, I drove home in numbness from the drink focused on nothing else but the road ahead and my destination.

Sunday morning, my head still numb from the night before, I woke to the sound of Pappa roaring in anger from the backyard. The tires to his truck had all been slit. Thousands of dollars were out the door! Who would do this and why? It was not long before I heard rumor in town that my brother was bragging about what he had done. He had followed me home, discovering where we lived, and disabled Pappa's only source of income.

Hearsay was not enough to catch him. He got away with the crime. Pappa fell into depression, unable to pay the household bills. He was forced to decide between putting money into the equipment or putting money into the house.

I had been saving money to make a trip to France to see Fabrice. We wrote constantly and called each other when we could afford the long-distance calls. I had saved three thousand dollars in preparation for the trip. Pappa never asked, but that money needed to be used to pay the bills and keep a roof over our heads.

I was never able to pool that kind of money again. I had moved to the city to attend college. Bills meant less disposable income. Still Fabrice and I wrote and called making plans, although our plans could never quite come together.

My older brother had also moved to the city to attend college. We tried to make a truce and heal things. There were good days and bad days, as we struggled through the pain of our childhood.

LIFTED UP

North Idaho College was in Coeur d'Alene. I enrolled selecting classes to move me toward work as a clothing designer, one of my childhood dreams.

Mom would make the trek from Montana to North Idaho to bring supplies, food, bedding, dishes, and clothes. Most trips, I had no idea she had been there. I would hear about it once she was gone. I was not graced with her visits or her supplies. That old feeling of being unwanted and of not being enough came crashing back in like a tidal wave.

One weekend while drinking and dancing with my friends, I was told how my brother was bragging about the music and other items he had taken from me. Filled with courage from the drink, a friend and I, made our way to his apartment. Nerves firing, we snuck into his complex, and found his car, that was a hatchback with a "wing" window. His car locked tight, I peered through the window and saw my Canadian music tapes strewn across the passenger seat.

We devised a plan to retrieve my belongings. Very carefully, I slid the screwdriver under the glass, prying slowly. The window was moving! Impatience took over, and one twist too hard ended in the ring of glass shattering. Oh hell! I unlocked the door, grabbed my items, hopped back in our getaway car, and sped off.

It was not long before the police came knocking. Interrogation time. I was held for more than 12 hours being interrogated. I stuck to my denial. I spent the day being threatened and intimidated. Fists pounded on the table in front of me. Louis had told them that the music was his, but he upped the ante adding several other items to the list including a couple hundred dollars in cash. What would have been a misdemeanor had quickly been worked into a possible felony!

I broke in the late hours of the evening and admitted to what I had done, but only to breaking the window and the music tapes. I told about living in Canada and how he had stolen the tapes from me. I had to pay for his window, but the felony charges were dropped after a lengthy lie detector test.

Our delicately balanced relationship was upturned once again. Of course, Louis and Mom directed all the blame at me. I was filled with a mix of burning rage and searing disappointment. My ulcers threatened their return. Depression found one more footing in my heart and mind. One more time, I felt I had been wronged. Yet, I was the one being punished. Would it ever end? Would I ever be enough?

College was filled with more friends, partying, and adventures. I made friends with the basketball players and even dated one or two. Basketball games were tricky. I wanted to go hang out with friends and watch, but my brother was often there. His anger at me had increased to pure hatred. I avoided the games most nights.

One Friday night, a team that one of my childhood friends and crushes was playing on was in town. Gathering up all the courage I could muster, I stepped into the gym. Spotting friends in the distance, I headed to where they sat and took my perch amongst them. Nearly as soon as I had taken my seat, whispers began, then warnings. My brother was in the crowd. Friends huddled around me in protection.

Catcalls and profanity came booming across the gym, directed at me. I felt shame, fear, and the need for the invisibility cloak that I had constructed in my mind. My physical form began to shrink, sitting on the bleachers.

Half time could not come too soon. Stepping down to the court, I greeted my childhood friend and apologized for the ruckus and the need to leave. Hugs, oh so needed hugs, were warmly given. He understood but had to get to the locker room.

Watching him walk away, I waved goodbye to my friends, weaving myself into the crowd headed to the door.

LIFTED UP

Cool fresh air! The black night sky and northern air greeted me as I stepped out of the gym. Focused on scurrying to my vehicle like a scared mouse, warning shouts fell across me. Too late! There he was, my older brother, coming at me. His hands closed around my neck so quickly I had no time to react.

A swarm of friends, his and mine, came rushing at us, prying his hands from my throat. He swung wildly at them, shouting more profanity at me. This time the profanity included death threats. Looking into his eyes, I had no doubt that he would have finished that threat had others not intervened. Basketball games were no longer an option for me. Watching my back and my every step became a daily habit.

A whirlpool of emotion, anger, frustration, fear, embarrassment, inferiority, insecurity, and depression filled me and began to take root deep within. Except for Pappa, I felt so unloved, so unwanted, and so unnecessary to my family. It's a feeling I pray you never have to feel.

It was my brother's last semester at college. Soon I would be safe, as soon as he took his leave of that city. Soon after his departure, strangers began to approach me. One by one, I was asked for drugs—for things I had no idea of what they were.

I had heard of them, but I really did not know the difference between marijuana, cocaine, or heroin. I would learn soon enough. I did not partake, but I had to learn because of all the requests coming at me. Finally, I asked why people kept hounding me about buying drugs. Word had gotten out that I was Louis' sister. He had provided them with the requests, and they figured maybe I had taken over when he left.

I was horrified! Confusion once again came swarming in. I was aware of some things about my brother, but nothing could have prepared me for that news. Even through all the trauma, pain, and anger, I loved him. He was my brother—my family. (Isn't it odd how victims cling to their abusers?)

I was not innocent. I had my own issues. The rage and insecurity in me built and manifested in ways that made no sense at the time. One outlet was simple—sex. Arriving at college, I ran into childhood friends, boys who told me that they had wanted to date me in school but were too terrified of my older brother to approach me. He had threatened to kill anyone who came near me. Obviously, they were just as scared of him as I was.

All this time, I had thought I was just as unattractive as Mom had pounded into my head. It was the excuse that I built why I never went to prom, was never asked out, and was never paid attention to like the other girls. That notion dug its roots deep and still haunts me today.

It was oddly freeing. I took joy in the attention. I explored the possibilities of being wanted and of being found attractive. It's fair to say I abused the newfound freedom and did so for years to come.

My other outlet was shoplifting. Some angry corner inside me was convinced that I deserved more. I understand now how those actions are just a cry for help and how the depression and abuse culminated in a skewed sense of reality.

Of all the times I committed the crime, the one time that put a stop to it came at the price of a greeting card and a bottle of nail polish.

The sun was shining. I was bored. I was frustrated. I was hurt! Mom had come to town again and not bothered to see me. Irrationally, I headed to the drugstore to "shop". Exiting the store, secure in the fact that I was safe, I headed to my car. Hands on the keys to the car, opening the door, voices came booming behind me, "Stop! Stop right there!" My purse was emptied, and the items discovered. I was caught!

Orange jumpsuit lay across my arm, I stood for an unexpected photoshoot before being taken to change. My belongings were placed in a basket, whisked away, and locked up. I was allowed a phone call. Pappa! I never questioned his love. Embarrassed, my voice quivered as I told him what had happened and where I was. He offered no help! His voice was filled with disappointment. I had made the mistake, and I would pay the price. I made my bed, and I could now lay in it for the weekend.

Counseling with a local pastor, restitution, and check-ins with the authorities followed. It was arduous, but I was thankful for it. Thankful it was stopping. I never liked that I felt the need to shoplift. I certainly did not have the knowledge or coping skills to understand it. It never happened again. More than the embarrassment and disappointment in myself, I could not bear disappointing Pappa.

Stunned, I sat across the big messy desk of my college counselor. I had been called to her office unexpectedly. In another trip I was not told of, Mom had been in to the office to report me.

The counselor began to unfold a tale told her by my mother—a tale of drugs, theft, and prostitution. Apparently, I was paying my way through college by selling drugs and working as a hooker. Horror! How the hell could my own mother come and tell these lies to the college?

I shrank inside myself a little more that day. Another nail in the "I am not enough" structure being built in my mind was driven home. The pain that day caused is impossible to describe. Darkness fell over me. Alone in my apartment, I threw myself on my bed and wailed until morning. What had I ever done in life to deserve all this? My brother was selling drugs NOT me!

Gathering myself, I confronted her about the conversation. She never denied it, only justified it. I retorted that my brother was selling drugs not me! I was called delusional and accused of deflecting my transgressions on my brother.

Devastated, I could no longer focus. College was no longer an option for me. I was unable to finish my classes, and I left the city.

MISHA FAYANT

CHAPTER 11

NIGHTMARES AND LIES

*"There are many who don't wish to sleep for fear of nightmares.
Sadly, there are many who don't wish to wake for the same fear.'*
Richelle Goodrich

Hiding from the chaos over the last year, I moved to the country with Pappa in the North Idaho woods. An undeveloped forest plot became our new home. For a short time, I shared a back bedroom with my sister. We inhabited a singlewide trailer home placed in those woods.

Utilities and water were not installed when we first moved deep in the woods. We used a generator for power and large elevated tanks for water until we could drill a well. A new adventure! Pappa finally let me get back on the caterpillar dozer by then clearing the land and making our homesite.

Working at a local convenience store, I saved enough money to buy an 8-foot by 36-foot trailer to call my home. With Pappa's help, we hauled it to his property and placed it behind his trailer.

Water was one of our biggest needs. We spent our afternoons walking the property "witching" in search of water. The strongest indication causing the wires to downturn was found past my little trailer in the woods. A drilling rig was brought in and the quest for water began. Watching the beast of a machine drilling, pounding, whirring, and slamming through the rock base beneath us was mesmerizing.

The nightmares from my childhood had never ceased. They visited me every night. Now with the recent events and conflicts, wounds, fears, and frustrations, there were fresh nightmares to add to the library of darkness that held my nights captive.

"I still have the nightmares. I still see the same person who tortured me in my dreams."
Maher Arar

Deafening thumping and pounding could be heard outside my trailer. Waking delirious to find darkness, I hopped out of bed confused. It's the middle of the night! Why would the drilling rig be running at this hour?

I threw on clothes from the disheveled pile near my bed in haste. The night greeted me as I stepped out to find Pappa. What's going on? Why on earth are you running the rig this late?

Then I saw her. Bound and gagged. Mom had come to the property and threatened to kill me.

Before I could say a word, he tossed her in the hole being dug for the well. The drilling rig pounding down on her like a monstrous mixer, she was chopped into pieces. I stood frozen in fear, holding back the contents of my stomach demanding release.

LIFTED UP

Using Big black garbage bags, he was scooping her up into the bags! One-by-one, they were placed into the backseat of my car as I stood and watched confused, sick, and in terror.

"Get in and drive!" Pappa commanded. Numb, I did as I was told. Racing away in the dark, Mom's dismembered body was in trash bags in the back seat. Pappa was growling about how she would never harm me again.

From the rear-view mirror, I could see something moving. What on earth? Mom! She was reassembling piece by piece from those garbage bags. Her bloody hand was reaching over the seat grasping for me. Shrill but guttural sounds came from her mouth, letting me know she would kill me, and she would not stop until it was done!

I woke to a cold sweat, tremors, and tears. It was yet another nightmare. Lying in bed relieved that it was not true, I held back the heat in my stomach. Why was it like this? Why could she not ever love me? Was I such a horrible girl that she hated me so?

Her vengeance would not end with defiling me to the college; she tracked me down once again.

The sweetest young woman with dark hair, big eyes, and a sweeping smile hired me to work at a local convenience store. She was understanding and oddly protective of me.

Arriving at work one afternoon soon after that nightmare, she called me to her office. Immediately my mind went to panic mode. What was I in trouble for? What had I done? She closed the door behind her, took a seat, and looked at me with sad eyes.

Mom had come to the store. She had sought out my employer to tell her the same stories that were told to the college counselor. Seriously? Why would she not leave me alone? It was all lies. Thankfully, my employer knew Pappa and knew a little of our history.

MISHA FAYANT

She had been warned about Mom. She did not believe the stories, but she wanted me to know what had happened.

Depression was sinking deeper into my heart, even as I smiled bright on the outside. Hiding my pain had become a coping mechanism. Ashamed and broken, I did not want others to see what I carried inside me. I could not bear the disappointed eyes looking back at me if they ever found out how pitiful I really was. My light struggled to shine through as my hope of ever being loved by anyone but Pappa slowly eroded away.

An attempted robbery late at night at gunpoint was all I could take. Feeling unsafe from all sides, I knew I had to leave the convenience store in search of new employment. Keytronics, a computer keyboard company, had just opened a manufacturing facility in town. An industrial park was being built behind one of the local mills, and it inhabited the largest building standing. It would be my next place of employment.

A small trailer park perched on a hilltop overlooking the river was the new home for my little trailer. It was not much, but it was my home! A new job and my new home with running water and electricity gave my soul a little light in those dark days.

I found assembly work to be tedious and boring, but it was work and good income for a girl in North Idaho. I discovered a whole new set of people and experiences there. It felt like half the county was employed in that building.

I saw faces I knew, including the blond wrestler from high school who had stolen my heart years before. Also, faces I had never seen before showed up for work. Among them, an olive skinned, dark haired young man with big brown eyes and a moustache perched on his lip. I was immediately entranced with him. Flirting awkwardly and vying for his attention, I wanted to get to know him.

We started dating, and then moved in together. We sold my tiny trailer and moved into a larger one rented to us by the park. He introduced me to a different life. He drank daily, and he smoked weed. Watching him night after night with his pipe and the resulting calm that fell over him, I finally decided to give it a try.

So relaxed, I lay back on the couch, head wrapped in a cloud. My mind is an explorative thing, going a million miles an hour in a hundred different directions. This only amplified for me with the influence of marijuana. A numbness crept up my body starting in my toes and slowly working its way up my legs, then abdomen, chest, and neck towards my head.

Irrationally, my mind said that if that numbness reached the top of my head, I would die! Slowly it would make its way toward my eyes, and every time I would force myself up in a panic. This occurred over and over. My body would relax completely, then being forced ridged and painful at attention, only to fall prey to the creeping numbness again.

A pain in my belly urging the need to pee drove me to make my way to the bathroom, bumping walls in the hallway like a pinball in a machine. Sitting on the toilet, I stared at the wood paneling surrounding me on every wall in the small room. Faces and figures began seeping out of the walls, looming toward me.

My whole night was spent trying to find safety from the demons that inhabited my mind and soul. Demons who were released by the drug that had taken down the wall of resistance I had kept in place for so long.

I realized that I carried too much damage and held too expansive an imagination to handle the drug. It was clear the drug was not for me!

Frustration began to grow as he spent every day drinking alcohol and smoking marijuana. I may never know what he was trying to escape.

Days and nights came and went, as I had to pick his face up out of a bowl of soup to keep him from drowning in it. Undressing him like a baby before bed became routine. I would find him naked, standing under a tree that stood outside our door in nothing but his socks urinating. In his state, he had bypassed the bathroom and stumbled out the door.

Each passing day, it became clearer that we were mismatched. Arguments and fights broke out.

Eventually, my dream of him fell away. I expected to break up at any time. Instead, he proposed. Now what? My family, his family, and our friends all expected us to marry. My grandma was worried. I was one of the last from my graduating class to still be single and childless. With such pressure, I accepted his proposal. Inside, I kept praying for release from this commitment or for some miracle to retrieve me from it. There was no strength left in me to fight the expectations of friends and family.

I had one more hopeful thought. If I married, Mom would be wrong about no one wanting me. If I married, I would be somehow acceptable to her. (The broken mind makes no sense.)

The next 6 months were anything but bliss. Sexual activity between us stopped almost immediately after the proposal. I kept thinking something would happen and this would not be my future.

The messages from Mom about not being enough, not being wanted, not being loved, and no one ever wanting me pushed me forward. Part was the fear of her being right and part anger and wanting to prove her wrong. I dove headlong into wedding planning.

Plans were made to visit Montana in an attempt to reach out to Mom and include her in the plans. I wanted to try to gain approval, love, something! The day we arrived, steely cold greeted us at the door as we were told to go upstairs and wait. She did not have time to babysit us. He wanted to turn and leave immediately. I begged him to stay. We spent the day almost entirely alone. She was too busy to spend time with me or to meet my fiancé.

He was furious. He knew of the troubles between her and me. He saw the spite directed at me. He could not fathom a mother treating a daughter in this way. Immediately, he disliked her.

She had been integral in the planning of both my brothers' weddings. The western wear shop from my high school days had been transformed into a bridal shop. She provided them with dresses, tuxedos, flowers, and planning. We had limited funds. Gut churning once again, hands trembling, and voice shaking, I reached out to her for help. I would pay. Holding out hope to at least be able to find a dress at cost, a tuxedo for him, or flower—, anything would help.

I was denied. She told me to find something in Idaho. "I'm sure you can find a dress cheaper there." Tuxedos? She had hundreds in the basement she owned. Could we rent any of those to help with cost? "It would be too much hassle. Find something in Idaho" was the response yet again. It was made clear that we were welcome to purchase anything else we needed at the posted price, the same as any other customer.

"Every word, facial expression, gesture, or action on the part of a parent gives the child some message about self-worth. It is sad that so many parents don't realize what messages they are sending."
Virginia Satir

Gut punched! The message was clear to me. I still was not enough and was not wanted. It had been this way my whole life. Anything for the boys, and yet my requests were most often denied. The boys had gone to basketball and football camps. Excited at the news, I had asked when I was going. Scoffing at me, I had been told there was no money for me to do any of those things.

At the end of the day about a half an hour before we had to leave, she finally came up to say goodbye. It was the most uncomfortable and deflating visit.

Back in the car, he and I both were filled with an array of emotion. One thing was clear. He did not want her to be a part of the wedding. He was seething in anger, anger toward her he never overcame.

Plans continued, and invitations were printed. We decided that the invitations would state that his parents and my Pappa were announcing our wedding. She was not to be included on them because of that day, the day she turned me away yet again, and disrespected my husband-to-be.

Of course, it angered her. I'm sure it hurt her. Her vengeance with me was renewed. She told her family—my aunts, uncles, and cousins—they were not allowed to attend. She even made plans for a reunion to occupy the family that day, so they would not come to my wedding.

I could foresee those things happening. Of course, the damage needed to be taken a step further. One day, she made her visit to my mother-in-law to be. She sought her out at her place of employment. Unannounced, she demanded time with her.

Mom wildly stated she had to give a warning and told stories about me. My future mother-in-law said the stories were too horrible to repeat. They made her ill to her stomach and made her question what kind of mother would say such things about their daughter.

She told my future mother in-law that I was only marrying him for his money. My mother-in-law to be drank that night, something I rarely saw her do. Unfortunately, the seed had been planted. The doubt that would later help destroy things was placed in her mind and oh-so-close to home for me.

My wedding day came, and no one from Mom's side of the family attended. While it was expected, expectation did not buffer the hurt any at all.

My new husband and I took up the spare bedroom of my in-law's house for a short time while we began building our own house across the highway and up the hill.

I had begun smoking cigarettes in college to be cool. My new husband smoked as well. I am sure we both reeked of smoke. As is typical with smokers, we did not realize how much we smelled of smoke.

It became too much for my mother-in-law to bear. We never smoked in the house, but the smoke from our clothes infested the house. We moved into a camper outside the house to gain privacy and give her relief from the stench.

She complained of "that funny smoke" referring to marijuana. Fueled with the doubt Mom had placed in her by the stories told, she blamed me. Of course, it could not be her son smoking weed, and if he did, it was my fault and influence that caused it. Yet again, blamed for something I did not do, my self-worth eroded a little more.

The cracks in relationships with my new family began occurring one-by-one after Mom's visit. As we built our home, I was there every day working. I helped with anything that I could do! Hauling block for the basement. Dipping in hot barrels of tar to paint the basement walls and waterproof them. Helping frame the structure. Overcoming my fear of heights to help with the roof. Painting the exterior.

The tar in the searing hot barrel neared the bottom, and I could no longer reach it. I was heavy chested and feared my breasts dragging in the hot tar clinging to the sides of the barrel if I leaned into the barrel far enough to reach the remnants left. Timidly and cautiously approaching my father-in-law, I asked for help. Immediately I was loudly chastised as being lazy and helpless by my husband and father-in- law in front of friends gathered to help.

OUCH. Here we go again. New situation, same story the story of my life. I was striving to be seen and to be accepted only to be degraded at every turn.

Hurt and anger returned. What the hell? My husband's sister and her husband were building a house at the same time. She did not dirty her hands with any of the work I was doing. She simply swept up sawdust and cleaned up messes as they were made. It was okay for her to do nothing, and yet I'm working my ass off, and I'm lazy? Would I ever escape this kind of judgement? Maybe everyone else was right. I was worthless.

A battle continued raging inside me. The messages of not enough juxtaposed to Pappa's eternal belief in me. It was torturous.

The happy go lucky man I agreed to marry became increasingly angry and controlling behind closed doors. I acted out in the only ways I irrationally could. I spent money! Food and spending became my tranquilizers. This fueled his anger further. We fed off the worst parts of each other.

Attempting to escape my presence, he would go out drinking with friends. Drinking and smoking weed until early hours of the morning, our early days were already uncomfortable. Sex became almost non-existent between us.

I was married, and my needs were being met less than ever. Constant fights over finances, his drinking, and our sex life riddled our days. On one occasion I spewed out, "My dad is 60, and he gets more than I do!" Of course, this did not help. We were dysfunctional to say the least.

LIFTED UP

Despite our dysfunction, I wanted children so badly. We just were not able to conceive. A laparoscopy was performed because I had abdominal pain, and multiple cysts were found on my female organs. Medication was prescribed, and we were informed it would be difficult for me to conceive.

Every few weeks, I made the trek to Sandpoint, 45 minutes to the East of us, to visit the doctor. His office required me to drive by the courthouse. My sister-in-law worked there. As luck would have it, her window overlooked the street below. She would report later that I spent all our money on multiple trips to Sandpoint. His family had no knowledge of the medical challenges I was facing. The assumption of the worst was based on those seeds planted by Mom years earlier.

On holidays, we spent the day at his parents' house, us women in the kitchen cooking and cleaning, the men drinking and playing pool. Sister and Mother-in-Law would exclude me, not speaking when I was present and whispering behind my back at every opportunity. The weight of unacceptance began collapsing my heart. Eventually, I made excuses of being "sick" on those days, so I would not have to attend and face more of the seething disapproval that I had so long waited to escape from childhood.

Nights left home alone and not knowing where he was, I turned to heading out with a friend to the bars in town, dancing, drinking, and flirting. Offers were made, and there were attempts to get me to fall into infidelity. These offers were tempting, as my wounded soul yearned for attention. A kiss, it felt so right and yet so wrong. Pushing away, I stumbled to the car and headed home, sick at the thought of what I had almost done.

Depression and mental anxiety do not always show clearly. My issues from childhood, the nightmares, the memories, and that feeling of never being enough began clouding my head. Struggling to make out what was real and what was fantasy or nightmare, my husband began to worry about my mental state.

MISHA FAYANT

LIFTED UP

CHAPTER 12

ABANDONMENT ISSUES

"They say that abandonment is a wound that never heals.
I say only that an abandoned child never forgets."
Mario Balotelli

The room was dark and quiet, a sliver of light shone through the blinds in a window across the room. In the room was a simple, well-worn bed. Soft, quiet sobs emanated from the floor near the bed. A small shape dressed in a dirty light-colored nightgown curled in on herself, huddled close to the bed. Drawing closer, the ripple of tearstains across an unclean little face could be made out in the dim light. The quivering little girl looked up just enough to make eye contact for only a moment. Then a voice came on the television saying something about children left home alone.

That all too familiar ache began to grow in the pit of my stomach. That deep, dull, burning pain that preceded the need to vomit. My head would feel full and dense, spinning like a top out of control. Every time that old commercial would come on the television, I would have to step away. The emotions would become too intense.

Some days, depending on my state of mind and mood, I would end up in the bathroom. Kneeling on the cold tile, grasping the chilly porcelain bowl, I would heave repeatedly until I collapsed, tears of my own rolling down my cheeks in warm contrast to the room around me.

At first, I thought it was just my own deep sensitivity to the thought or sight of children being hurt, neglected, abused, a deep empathic thing. As a young adult in my 20's, I struggled to make sense of my extreme sensitivity to the sights and sounds of these commercials or scenes in movies and television shows. I thought that maybe it was just because I was so naïve, so sheltered.

"I grew up in a confused house: too much unwanted attention or none at all."
Mary Oliver

As I stepped on my long journey to healing, and self-empowerment, I began to realize the truth. Poor Pappa was once again confronted. We had become used to our talks. I was far more comfortable asking questions as old wounds were explained and as my self-confidence returned.

He told me of how I had often been left alone at home just like that little girl. I felt so bad for Pappa having to relive all this, having to explain to the little girl that he so wanted to protect but could not so many times. More and more pieces would be thrown onto the table of the puzzle that was my story.

It was early. There was still a chill in the Northern Idaho air, as I pulled the blankets up over my head trying to grab one last moment of warmth. Mom's voice rang out from the other room calling for me to get up, "You have swim class this morning, and I have things to do! Let's get going!" she chimed.

MISHA FAYANT

I loved swimming lessons. I loved water. It was my joy spot as a child! We lived outside of town far from anywhere to swim. The trips to the pool on the South Hill of our little town were always exciting for me. It was a magical place to be, a place I wished I could be every day.

This morning, though, we headed out earlier than normal, and my brothers were not along for the trip that day. Mom and I packed into our car and drove to town. She was excited, a little agitated, clearly in a hurry, and thinking about other things—her day ahead or whatever she had to be doing for the day.

We pulled up to the pool while the sun was just beginning to rise over the hill, dew still on the grass, and a nip in the air. She told me to get my things and hurry up, as she had to get going.

I was confused. No one else was there. What was I supposed to do? She told me to make sure I attended my swim lesson and do what I was told. Then she pointed to a spot on the lawn outside the chain link fence surrounding the pool and told me to wait for her there.

She said I was not to go anywhere else, and that I had better be right in that spot when she returned. I had a small snack for breakfast, but no food or water other than that. I got out of the car and grabbed my towel and swimsuit, thinking she would be back shortly after my lesson.

It was at least a half an hour before anyone else showed up to let me into the locker room of the pool. By then I was just so excited to be able to swim that nothing else registered in my young mind.

After the lesson was done, I changed into dry clothes and took up post on the grass outside that was just beginning to dry from the morning dew. My friends were there, and I was oblivious to much except the post that I had promised to keep, and the fact that I was laughing, playing with my swim friends, somersaults and cartwheels on that uneven hillside, tumbling in the grass in the warm summer sun.

LIFTED UP

My stomach began to gnaw from hunger, and my tongue became thick and dry from dehydration. The other kids were all gone from their lesson, and I was now alone on the hill. Strangers came and went, playing in the pool. I was too scared to leave my post and get into trouble to go back in and swim.

When I decided I had to get something to drink, panic ran through my bones, like cold steel. I was terrified of leaving that prescribed spot in the grass, but I was so thirsty! I ran inside to get a drink. Shaking the entire time, I hurried as quickly as I could to return to my towel on the lawn.

I had no cover, and I was not going to go sit in the shade of the trees for fear of being found in a spot that I was not supposed to be in. The sun beat down on me all day. I could feel my skin warming, and then turning to unbearable heat. Still I held my post in fear.

I sat there all day on that spot on the grass, waiting for her to return. No food, no water, no shelter, no sunscreen. My skin was starting to bubble from the burns developing across my shoulders and legs.

The sun went down slowly and the temperature with it, steadily moving from that scorching heat to a welcome evening cool, to an all too chill northern summer night. Still I sat in that one spot. Now there was no one left. There had not been for hours. I was starting to feel scared, not of the anger of Mom from not being where I was supposed to be, but from the dark, from being alone, and the unknown.

Curled over my knees, shaking from the cold and trembling from the copious number of tears now steadily covering my face, I heard footsteps in the grass behind me. I turned and asked, "Mom! Is that you?" but I recognized that it was not. It was a stranger, and in that moment, the fleeting feeling of relief turned into a sudden panic.

Frozen solid from the fear of an unknown figure walking toward me in the dusk, I heard a soft voice. As the woman neared, I could see the look of concern on her face. Still I pulled away from her outreach knowing that I was not to talk to strangers.

She was persistent, calm, loving, and asked if I was hungry and if I needed something to drink. "I live in that house right there," she said pointing over her shoulder to an open door across the street. "I have been watching you all day. Where is your Mother?" she asked quietly.

"I don't know," I replied through the calming sobs.

"Let's go to my house, and I will fix you something to eat," she urged softly.

"I can't!" I exclaimed, "Mom told me to wait right here and not to move. I can't go!"

The woman knelt next to me and said, "You have been a good girl and waited right at that spot all day, just like you were told. But it is night now, and you cannot stay out here alone in the dark." She slowly stood up, taking my hand, and led me to her house reassuring me the whole time that it would be okay. I would not be in trouble.

Once in her house, she fed me, had me drink water over and over and started applying cool packs to my shoulders and legs that were now deep red and blistered. It was now after 9 PM.

Just as I began to get comfortable and drift off to sleep on the couch in her small living room, there was a knock at the door. I heard my mother's voice. It was urgent and angry. She thanked the woman for taking care of me and jerked at my hand pulling me out the door mumbling under her breath, "I told you not to move! What were you doing in her house, you don't even know her!"

Once in the car, doors shut, driving away, I was backhanded over and over again, rants and screams rushed over me all at once. She was angry over me making her look bad, not doing what I was told, not being where I was supposed to be, and for being stupid and

LIFTED UP

bratty. I was grounded and unable to leave the house. At home, I was spanked with a belt and told to get to bed. I only remember a canvas of hands and words flying at me until I fell into bed sobbing and unable to sleep from the pain of my well-fried skin.

The stories continued, as I grew older I began feeling more like a pawn than a loved child.

I was athletic, even though I was "heavy, fat, and unattractive". I loved sports and was very competitive. I played soccer when I was young, even some softball, but as I grew into a teenager, it became volleyball, basketball, and also track and field.

I had worked hard to prove myself, always hoping that if I achieved more I would be seen and acknowledged, but it just never seemed to happen.

One Saturday, I had been playing in a basketball tournament in Coeur d'Alene. I watched all day long for her face in the crowd, but it never came, not until the tournament was over. I went to the front of the school and waited on the sidewalk. Finally, Mom drove up, impatient and in a hurry. She directed me to get into the car.

I asked her why she did not come to watch me play. The response was the usual. I was selfish, self-centered, and did not think of anyone but myself. I never got any answer as to why she did not watch me, when she made sure that she attended my brothers' games!

Then there was the time we traveled together to Spokane. The car ride had been long and tense. I was excited though to get to spend a day with Mom, to have an adventure, to be alone with her, and hopefully have fun and be acknowledged even a little by her.

Once we arrived at the outskirts of town, we pulled over at a truck stop off Sprague, she told me to go inside and wait. I was confused, but knew better than to question her, so I went inside and waited alone.

About a half an hour later she came back and gave me a key to a hotel, she told me to walk up the street and go straight to the hotel. I would be going in alone! She told me she had somewhere to be and did not have time to stay. The hotel was a few blocks away, and it was dusk. I was about 15, but timid in many ways, growing up in small town Northern Idaho.

She pulled up to the gas pumps and started to fill the tank. I waited but was soon firmly told to get moving and get to the hotel. She would not be driving me.

Those streets of Sprague were plagued with pimps and prostitutes during those days. I hurriedly walked toward the hotel blocks away. Soon a man began shouting at me and ran across the street to talk to me. He was asking my name, and what I was doing on the street at that time of day alone. I told him I was just walking to the hotel. He began making advances and asking if he could come with me. (I later found out he was a pimp).

Mom must have seen what was happening as she pulled away from the gas station, and she came roaring up in the car, yelling at me. I was so confused and scared, I knew that the man was not good, I could feel it in the pit of my stomach, and honestly, I was afraid I was about to be raped.

"And what if--what are you if the people who are supposed to love you can leave you like you're nothing?"
Elizabeth Scott

She had me get in the car yelling at me the whole time about how I could not do even the simplest thing right. She pulled up around the corner from the hotel and told me to get out. She said she had only paid for one person and that we could not be seen going in together.

I was to go in and lock the door, and not open it or go out for anything until she returned.

I ran to the door fumbling with the key I could not get inside quick enough. SLAM! The door flung shut behind me, and I locked it as tightly as I could. I pulled the curtains closed and sat in the chair in the corner away from the window and door, waiting for her, terrified, knowing that I was in prostitute alley.

We did not have cell phones back then, so there was no way to get a hold of her. She did not tell me where she was going, only that she was going to see an old lady in a home. I begged to go with her. She refused. I had no idea when she would return. I thought because of the time of day and who she said she was going to see, that she would be back in a few hours at most.

"When loneliness is a constant state of being, it harkens back to a childhood wherein neglect and abandonment were the landscape of life."
Alexandra Katehakis

I sat in that chair huddled up in fear, a sick feeling growing in my stomach with every passing hour, all night long and into the morning. She arrived the next morning and told me to hurry up and get ready to leave because we needed to go get breakfast.

We drove to the nearest IHOP and walked in. As soon as we entered a man with a large mustache that she hugged immediately greeted us. I thought it was odd the way she was acting. Even more odd, he sat with us, and she sat with him instead of by me in the booth at the back corner of the restaurant.

They were clearly flirting and mostly oblivious to me during the whole breakfast. I could tell she had her hand on his leg and confirmed it when I leaned over to pick up something I "dropped". Her and Dad were still married, and I had no clue there was any issue. I was sick and felt like I would throw up. How could she? Then it dawned on me why she left me all alone in that hotel, because she spent the night with HIM.

It was bad enough that I had looked forward to time with her, to time with the mother I loved needed, and wanted approval from so badly. The one time we had a chance to have some "girl time", and she ditched me in a prostitute infested hotel to go have an affair.

Even as an adult, these things would happen.

When my grandmother died, I made the drive from Idaho to Montana to be by her side and help her. I spent days working in her floral shop babies in tow, to help make floral arrangements for the funeral. I did my best to please her, to prove myself to her, to be that child that she loved and needed.

I thought I had finally done it, UNTIL my brothers arrived. As soon as they came, I was pushed aside, no longer spoken to, and it was as if I did not exist. After all those days of working long into the night helping her, I was tossed aside as soon as my brothers stepped foot in the house. I tried to smile and insert myself into conversation and activities but was blocked and pushed aside at every move.

Finally, I was told to take the van and take the flowers to Kalispell, where the funeral would be held. It was about an hour and a half drive. She kept the kids with her and sent me alone to go to the funeral home.

Grandma was the rock for me in that family. Her loss was

immeasurable to me. I cried the whole way to town, wiping my tears away as I pulled up to the funeral home. I unloaded the many arrangements and then was allowed to go view Grandma alone. No one was there to console or comfort me. After all I had done and all I tried to do, it was not enough, still never enough.

I then had to go to the church for the funeral. Arriving at the church, I saw my family sitting near the front, Mom, my two brothers and their wives sitting all in a row. When I approached, I was told there was no room for me and I was to sit elsewhere, even though there was clearly space for me to take a seat. I sat alone, two rows behind my family in grief over the loss of my Grandmother and in grief over being pushed aside once again.

At the reception after, I tried to approach and be a part of the family. Backs were turned and everything I said was ignored, except for my younger brother who tried to include me. It was painful to be there, to have worked so hard to be the daughter I thought she wanted, and to still be so coldly pushed aside. I'm not sure if she even acknowledged what she was doing or if it had just become so routine that she no longer noticed.

"Abandonment doesn't have the sharp but dissipating sting of a slap. It's like a punch to the gut, bruising your skin and driving the precious air from your body."
Tayari Jones

Years later, I made the trek again to visit for a cousin's wedding. Walking in, close family recognized me, cousins, aunts, but anyone outside of that circle did not know who I was. I was asked by one person how I was related (a cousin of my mom's). When I explained who I was, they said no, that is impossible, she has only one daughter, and they pointed to my younger sister. I was told she never spoke of me. In all the many years none of them knew I even existed.

I wore a fashionable dress that day, trying to look as perfect as possible. Though many others told me that I looked amazing, the one person I wanted praise from told me that I looked fat and dressed like a prostitute. That day I was not spoken to outside of those comments and turned and made the long drive back to Idaho. The comments about my appearance made me feel dirty and small. The conversations with distant family made me feel foolish, unwanted, and an outcast. How does your own mother never speak of you? In nearly 30 years, no one even knew I existed outside of immediate aunts, uncles, and cousins.

I changed out of my dress as I drove. I felt so foolish for thinking that I would appear poised and put together. I could not get out of it fast enough. Tears once again streaming down my face as I drove. It was hours to home, and I don't even know how I got there without some kind of ticket or accident. I was crushed. I wanted to crawl under a rock. I was furious! I was still not enough.

I have had abandonment issues all my life and for the longest time I did not realize why. I knew the stories of my life, but somewhere in the dysfunction, maybe as a coping mechanism I had started to separate out painful memories and set them aside as if they did not really belong to me. It was a twilight space created in my mind, a space between "these are my memories and they hurt like hell!" and "these are stories just like the many stories I read about or hear about, but not mine."

These issues have caused problems in all my relationships. I learned to expect that people would leave me.

LIFTED UP

"When you fully understand that as long as YOU are with you,
you will never feel totally abandoned."
Michelle Fayant

CHAPTER 13

BIRTH STORY

"She was born silent into this world,
but her little life spoke volumes."
Unknown

It had been a rough week. I was just learning to sort and cope with the stories of my life. Pappa was forced to begin to tell me pieces as I brought information, memories, and questions to him—questions that needed answers.

My parents had been divorced for more than a dozen years. I don't even remember what happened that particular day, but I had allowed hurt into my heart yet again over some misunderstanding with Mom. It was common. We would get along, then something would happen to open old wounds. Our relationship was rocky to say the least.

I had driven out to my Pappa's house. I visited that little country house a lot. It was my escape. I know that I had relayed a story to him of the last round of battles with her. Piercing blue eyes gazed back at me through indescribable pain. Sitting on that couch, chest heaving with labored breath and face soaked with fresh fallen tears, I asked him, "Why does she hate me so much? Why is nothing I ever do good enough? Why does she push me aside time and again? All I ever wanted is for her to love me."Calmly, solemnly, he took my hand and said, "Honey, I need to tell you something. When you were born, I was given an impossible choice," he said. "I was in the waiting room at the hospital. I paced and waited for a long, long time. It felt like an eternity, and I knew something was not right. Eventually the doctors came out to talk to me. They fumbled around like idiots and then they said to me, 'Mr. Fayant, we are sorry to tell you there are complications with the birth of this baby. The mother and baby are in danger. We can only save one of them. You must make a choice. Who do you want us to save? The mother or the baby?' I told them to save the baby."

He paused, took a long slow breath and continued, "You see, baby girl, in our heritage we believe that the parent has already had a life to live, but the child has a full life ahead, and so I chose you. It was the only thing I could do. She had already had a life, you had not."

He paused once again and looked into my eyes before continuing, "I went out to my truck and got my shot gun!" he exclaimed. "Then I went back into the hospital and found the doctors, I pointed that shot gun at them and told them, 'Now either THEY both live or one of YOU dies'."

He stopped, a small smile crept onto his lips and he continued, "They saved you both. But your mother knew I had chosen you over her, and she could not forgive that. I am sorry. I did the only thing I knew how to do. She only focused on the part that I chose you first. From that day on, I could see she treated you different than your brothers."

His eyes had dropped to the floor. "I am sorry. It's why I always tried to protect you and take you with me when I could." (He drove long haul truck when I was young, which meant he was gone days at a time.) He explained that the events of that day scarred her heart and made her jealous of me in some way.

That was the beginning of my life; the beginning of the story of me.

The beginning of the years of hurt, abandonment, and of never being enough for one parent and being "saved" time and again by the other. So much made sense now! But I was in my late 20's by then. The damage had been done. My subconscious had carved its reality deeply into my being. I had bought the story of not being loved and not being wanted.

I sat on the heavily worn old sofa facing Pappa sitting in his tattered leather recliner, in the long, narrow, tiny living room of that little house. I felt confused, yet relieved, and so conflicted. I wanted to have the same indifference for her that I felt she held for me, but it was not within me to feel that.

I instead strove to feel empathy, trying to understand what I would do. How I would react if my husband were to do the same with me? Would I understand his decision? Would I feel unloved by his decision? Would I be able to comprehend the impossible choice he had to make?

I remember feeling a burning hot pain in my stomach as I sat there working to digest the information I had just been given. My head spun like I was on a carnival ride. I thought I might throw up, and so I sat frozen for a time.

Finally, a light emerged in the back of my head as the message began to sink in. Acceptance of the story helped to heal a little bit of the deep wounds in my heart and psyche. It was something, anything that I could hold on to, in order to explain the many years of pain.

One by one, memories came flooding through that evening. One by one, those memories were re-sorted and filed according to the new information I had. It was the beginning of healing. The subconscious is a stubborn thing though, and so the events of my life continued to haunt me. They pulled me into years of deep depression and despair.

LIFTED UP

It took another 20 years and many more disappointments for me to begin to come to terms with the reality of those early events that would end up shaping my entire life. I tried so hard to understand her hurt and pain, and what it would feel like to be in her shoes. The reality is she was hurt and damaged just like me. She had events and stories in her own life that made her feel unwanted, unloved, and never enough in the eyes of her family.

She did not have the tools or the maturity to understand the triggers and change the way she must have felt every time she looked at me. She was young and doing the best that she knew how. I can see now that she tried to work hard to overcome, and in her own way, heal those things.

CHAPTER 14

LITTLE YELLOW HOUSE

*"I am not what happened to me.
I am what I choose to become."*
Carl Jung

My grandma and aunts lived in a town a few hours' drive away. We would go to visit Grandma often. Some days, we would visit her at work, running into the department store where she earned a living as a clerk. She was always so happy to see us. She was such a light for me. Grandma was one of my first heroes. Her love for me was above and beyond what I experienced from any other woman in my life.

Those trips to visit Grandma meant that we drove past a certain spot in town. In that spot, there was this little yellow house tucked against a hillside. Every time we drove by, I would get this feeling in my stomach that I could not place or explain. It was an emptiness, a coldness—like steel in my gut. Time and again, we drove by the house, and I would wonder why I felt the things I felt.

I felt as if I knew that house. I could smell the air in the house and see the dust particles floating in the still quiet of the light flooding in from a window in the bedroom. I could see the layout of the house and where the furniture was. It was stark inside, not many belongings no real decorations anywhere. I knew that house, but I had no idea

LIFTED UP

why. I had been having dreams and nightmares; almost nightly since before I was 5 or 6. In one recurring nightmare, I would be walking and then realize that there were men standing in rows, naked from the waist down, their man parts in hand. I was scared to continue, but even more frightened for what the repercussions would be if I did not. A distant, commanding male voice would make it clear that I would be forced to stay the course, walking right in front of the men. As I walked they would ejaculate on me over and over again.

The nightmare was vivid. I could see and describe their genitals, and the white streaming down over me thick and hot. As a young girl, although I did not know the term for it, I could describe it well and in clear detail. I had no idea why or how I knew these details that haunted me almost nightly until my 20's. I learned in time that it was not normal, and that a child that young should not know those details.

At the same time, there was another dream. A coyote man would come to our house and unabashedly walk straight to the front door and knock loudly. My mother would answer the door, and I could hear him asking for me. Each and every time, I was given to the man. I cried as he took me away, my Mom standing in the doorway watching without a word. He would take me to a hut or small house nearby, and most often right in the front yard of our home, where he would "make me his wife." He would force me to stay.

In the dream, I would yell and scream begging for someone to come help me. I would be held down and told to be quiet, tears streaming down and panic coursing through my bones. He would tell me that my mother knew and did not care and that I belonged to him, and there was nothing I could do about it.

In the nightmare, it felt as if it would never end. Inside the nightmare, I always wondered why no one came to save me when they knew what was happening and were close enough to hear my screams. Morning came, and I would be released, only to be returned each night to relive this "duty". This nightmare occurred regularly several times a week, many times every night, for about 15 years. Every night I was raped in the dream to be released in the morning and relive it each succeeding night.

"Once you are defiled, you can't get back your purity by any means, instead, you will only look for ways to be defiled over and over again."
Michael Bassey Johnson

I could never make sense of how a young girl of that age would know the intimate details of a man's anatomy or function in the way I was able to describe. It wasn't until years later that those answers started to filter in.

These nightmares happened until my mid 20's. It was at this age that I had gotten married. Now married, everything began crashing in. I felt as if I was going crazy. I had hazy dreams and nightmares that felt as if they were reality and not just an overactive mind. As more and more veiled memories came bubbling up, they demanded answers I did not have. I began to seek answers from my father—answers that did not come easily or comfortably for either of us.

One sunny, spring day driving through a small northern town, and talking with my then-husband about my childhood, I had a rush of emotion. I felt a compelling need to know what that house was and why I knew it so well. We were already driving out to see Pappa. When we arrived, I received my hugs from him—hugs that felt as if they saved my life each and every time.

It took some time to get up the courage to ask. I had spent so many years having everyone tell me I was just plain crazy. I no longer knew what was real, what was memory, and what was just dreams. I had

LIFTED UP

begun to ask Pappa questions about the dreams and nightmares. I asked because I told him they did not feel like dreams, they felt more like memories, and I was confused.

Pappa and I had a good relationship. For the most part, I felt I could tell him anything. Some things were still uncomfortable, and I hesitated, but I was at a point in life that for my sanity's sake, I needed answers. I needed a way to make sense of all the images flooding in day and night, all the feelings being evoked and triggered by simple things.

It seemed as if going to the grocery store and seeing an item on a shelf could trigger that gnawing in my gut that meant something was unresolved. Seeing a tree lean a certain way, seeing the sun peek through and cast a familiar glow—simple things could bring me to tears I could not explain or evoke panic I did not understand.

I fumbled, not knowing how to ask... I had been told so many times by others in my family how damaged and delusional I was. Finally, I got up the courage, with his support, to begin to talk to him vaguely about what I was seeing in my nightmares. I told him that I had been having them since we moved to Idaho from Montana. I was so young then, and they had continued all this time. I was confused and scared, but I told him that they oddly felt more like memories than just nightmares. I asked if he knew why I was having them and/or what they meant.

His face became solemn as I described what was going on. There was a look of horror on his face. His sparkling eyes went flat. His head dropped. His gaze fell to the floor. His shoulders slumped, and I could see him tremble. Then I heard something I rarely ever heard from him. Sobbing. Crying. I did not understand what was going on. I tried to comfort him and tell him that it was okay. They were just dreams, and I was just being "odd" again.

His head lifted. He wrapped his arms around me still shaking and sobbing. He held me tight and said, "I'm sorry, I'm so sorry." I pulled

150

back and asked him what was going on. He tried talking through his tears and told me, "I thought you would never remember. I hoped you would never remember. I thought you had forgotten and that you would be okay." Again, I asked him what was going on. What was he talking about? In the pit of my gut I knew, but I was too horrified to accept it.

He began to tell me a story. A story that pulled so many pieces of nightmares and memories together. Things I never told anyone. Things he would not, could not know that I remembered, because I never told a soul!

When I was a little girl younger than 5, he had been sick and bedridden. He had lived a trauma-filled life. He had been run over by a school bus in grade school leaving his feet maimed. I remembered that story. They had replaced pieces of him with silver, trying to reconstruct his bones. His toes wrapped over each other in a mangle.

Later as an adult, he fell deathly ill. The doctors could not figure out what was wrong with him. He was so ill, he was bedridden, and they thought he would die. Later, it was found that the silver in his feet was dissolving and poisoning his blood stream, making him so ill he should not have survived.

He said he and mom were having marital issues at the time as well. He could not work, so she had to work and provide for the family due to his illness. Our little home was a few miles out of town in the prairies.

According to him, during that time Mom would take me to town. He said that it was a cover that he did not catch on to for a while. She had a boyfriend in town that she visited often. Many times, she would leave me at his house alone with him. That little yellow house by the hill? THAT was his house. Still fighting back tears, he told me that he did not know for a while what was happening, but when he figured it out, he threatened the man and Mom.

LIFTED UP

He continued telling me about how she became so angry when she had been found out. This was the late 1960's. Some of the nation was starting to have some sexual revolution, but it was unheard of in the remote areas we lived in. Terrified of being made to look bad in front of family, church, and community, she hired a couple of prostitutes to say that Pappa had raped them. He was jailed and later released because there was no physical evidence against him. He told me she knew that her boyfriend had taken liberties with me. Much more began to make sense.

My dream/memories had involved a scene where I had gone to the jailhouse with Mom. She had taken my hand and led me into a large cold grey room and stood me in front of what I remembered as a metal "cage". A man came from behind the cage and led my Pappa into it. Locking him in, he had chains on his hands and feet. I was horrified. That was my Pappa! Why was he in the cage and chained up? I tried to run forward to him. Mom grabbed my arm firmly and held me back pulling me to her side. She said "No, you stay right here. THIS is what they do to men who rape women."

*"I know you may cringe when I mention my childhood sexual abuse
and I understand. The mere thought of an adult
harming a child in any way should make you cringe. BUT. . .
I will not stop talking about it, healing from it, and helping
others heal as well. I will keep talking about it because
it may just be YOUR child I save."
Reverend Brian Dell Beckstead*

I never told anyone that story. I thought it, too, was a bad dream, but now it made sense. The pieces of the puzzle started to fit together. So many images and feelings came rushing in. For a time, I felt buried under the rubble of all the pieces that came pouring down on me. That one answer was the shovel that I needed to begin to dig myself out and uncover myself from the years of lies and deceit.

Even with those answers, it seemed surreal as if it happened to someone else and not me. The nightmares eventually subsided, never to return. I received confirmation of some of the facts from outside parties. Out of fear and humiliation, I did not speak about it with anyone else. There were days I was able to stay detached from it all, and then there were the days I crumbled when I felt buried alive.

There was a duality in me as if I had a split personality. Part of me was naïve about men. I remember my first boyfriend. I would not even hold his hand, terrified of being touched, but wanting to be loved and liked.

In high school, I fell in love with a golden-haired boy with bright blue eyes. He was tall, athletic, and vibrant. He had charisma. He was a football player and a wrestler, and I was a hopeless geek new to town. When he began to flirt, and a boy noticed me, I nearly lost my mind. I would do anything to make him happy, and yes, I lost my virginity to him.

He had been seeing a different girl before me and told me they were broken up. It was not all true.

I felt so dirty. The next day at school I wore my jacket all day and would not look anyone in the eye. I was sure they could tell. I felt as if everyone was looking at me, judging me, and whispering behind my back about how filthy and disgusting I was.

Then there was my strict Christian religious background that added to that. I had been taught that any sexual conduct outside of marriage made me unclean. The message weighed on my heart, and I shrank a little bit from the rest of the world for months following.

LIFTED UP

It began a time of promiscuity. I went from being innocent to a wild pendulum swing in the opposite direction. As a teen, I just knew that I was being seen. I was noticed! I wanted so much to be loved; I threw myself into situation after situation. More than that, there was this odd need or drive for more sexually that I could not explain.

I heard about girls who had been sexually abused and how they tended to become promiscuous as a result. I knew something was not right, but I did not know how to contain it. It almost felt like a rebellion, one running out of control. After the story of my childhood was finally let out, it made more sense to me.

At the same time, it caused even more pain. I felt out of control, and I think part of me was so angry and rebellious that I just did not care. I did not want to deal with one more thing. I did not want to heal, I just wanted to be pissed off and act out! The problem was, the only person I was really hurting was me.

There are certain men who sense these traumas in young women and they take advantage of that pain and rage and broken psyche. It's like bees to honey. My life was scattered with them.

My work life was littered with stories of men who abused their power and position. Men who felt the crack in my soul, and tried to slither their way in. Men who attempted to cross good business lines and take what they saw was a young, fractured girl.

Some men sought to take advantage sexually, some men just saw the brokenness and exerted control in any aspect they could.

I married a man who seemed lighthearted and playful at first. The funny thing is our courtship was like a misty, muddy drama I looked at from the outside. I was shocked when he proposed. I kept thinking something would happen before the actual marriage, and we would not really get married. Part of me wanted to be married. (My family was calling me an "old maid" because I was 21 and unmarried!) Part of me begged for everything to fall through. I did not know how to say STOP. I did not know how to say NO. The wedding went on, and I found myself married.

He changed. (We both did). The pressure of marriage, financial responsibilities, and socio-economic expectations wore on him. He was an alcoholic. We tried so hard to function, but only brought out the devil in each other. He began to exert more and more control trying to contain his uncontained wife. I allowed more and more of me to be broken down and ripped away until I woke one day to a woman I did not recognize.

I looked in the mirror and was shocked at the overweight woman looking back at me through clouded eyes. I had never been tiny, but had not allowed myself to be so unkempt, so big, and so out of control. The daily threats, the tantrums, the abuse no one could see—wore on me until I was unrecognizable even to me.

I left him and struck out on my own--the two kids in tow. Eventually, I ended up moving to the city in hopes of creating more space between my ex and me. I also hoped to find a job that would pay enough for me to be able to support my kids and me.

I worked at a job for a local company that was comprised of three different divisions: a commercial construction, commercial property, and a personal property. I worked overseeing the commercial and personal-held properties for this company. It was a good job, but it kept me extremely busy.

The owner and I butted heads constantly. I was just rediscovering my strengths, my feminine power, and myself. To be honest, I always had somewhat of a strong personality. This man was used to being in control of women. The only other woman in the business who had more longevity than me happened to be his ex-wife, and she had an interest in the company.

It started out well enough. I had my strengths and my flaws, and so did he. I was strong, playful, a bit opinionated, and finding myself again as a single woman. He demanded full attention be on his business. In his opinion, a woman should not have a personal life. Her life should revolve around his business.

This was not something I assumed. This was something directly told me on multiple occasions. It was told to me in no uncertain terms that I was not to have a personal relationship or outside interests, and that my life was to be focused on my job and his business and that alone.

Somehow, I tended to end up working for the same type of man. Most of them were well educated with multiple interests in business, and most of them had a very particular view on a woman's place. I would never assume to say that I was without flaws in our dysfunctional work relationship. Looking back, I recognize that a lot of what I did every day in his business was my subconscious lashing out in rebellion against him, and every man who had harmed and controlled me.

His lack of complete control over me grated on his every last nerve. He would become volatile, often screaming and yelling at me. One time he even grabbed me and shoved me into a wall holding me there to unload his tirade. He was irate because I oversaw portions of a project, but a senior employee had come in and made changes— changes which he wanted to hold me accountable for. When I pointed out that I did not make the changes, he lost his temper. I was shocked that none of the men in the office stepped in, they just stood looking on--some in shock.

I was also frantically looking for a man to fill the gap in my post-divorce life. It was a time when I wore dresses and heels daily, had my nails done, and admittedly dressed more than somewhat provocatively, seeking the attention of men. I grew up in an era where a woman was not complete if she was not married.

Part of me knew and validated that I was fine on my own, another part of me panicked at the thought of being alone. I spent a lot of time outside of work chasing a relationship. Unfortunately, that panic lead me to spending some of my worktime communicating online with perceived prospects.

My boss suspected this, but could not prove it, and that drove his fury towards me even further. My state of mind at the time and my lingering martyrism allowed me to justify my actions in my own mind. I desperately wanted, needed, and sought out validation from someone, anyone, outside myself. He sensed that, sensed the weakness in me in that area, and began making comments that should have been considered sexual harassment. Actually, a couple of male co-workers made comment about the inappropriateness of the things he said towards me.

In all honesty, I was more than a bit wild at the time. I had just come out of an abusive marriage. My ex-husband made sure to let me know how unattractive and undesirable I was during our 15 years together. That was solidified for me in the fact that he preferred to spend more time with pornography than with me. Now I recognize it as his attempt at control, but at that time his opinions, his words as a man, cut to my core. I was on a self-destructive path to prove him wrong.

It was during this time that I allowed myself to fall into a world and an existence that was exciting and new. I met a man who I allowed to convince me that I was a submissive woman. He took me down the path to the world of BDSM (an acronym for bondage/discipline, dominance/submission, sadomasochism)

I wanted and needed approval and escape so bad that I was willing to accept anything if it meant that I was recognized. It was a strange and risky world that both intrigued me and offered some mental escape from my own world. The funny thing is that it was just mirroring the relationships I had already had more intensely. Control, abuse, and sexual objectification were rampant in that world. Even as all of this was going on, I recognized that it was driven from my experience as a child. I knew somewhere deep down inside my mind that all of

LIFTED UP

this sexuality, this need for attention in that way, linked back to being mishandled by a man when I was very young. Part of me knew that as a survivor of sexual abuse, I would tend to be overtly sexual and seek out attention in this way. Still, that subconscious programming was stronger than my rational mind.

At one point, I even dreamed of writing a series of books based on my interactions in that world. I was so deep in denial and the comfort of what I was programmed to be that I did not want to find a way out.

I ended up seeing a man who took advantage of my lack of self-esteem and self-worth. I allowed myself to be back in the same swirling mess of abuse and degradation, but it had a new name! So now It meant it was okay, right? At least for a time, I convinced myself of that.

On our last "visit" together, I had angered him, so I was punished until my throat bled. When I was finally able to tear myself away (more like when he was finished with me), I gathered my things and ran away crying, tears falling so hard they were more blinding then the torrents of spring coastal rain coming down outside.

That night, driving home in the dark, rain pouring down, tears streaming down, I stopped several times to relieve myself of the burning pain in my gut.

Kneeling in the cold, wet muddy banks of the roadside, I wretched and struggled to gain my breath back. My throat in so much pain and blood still salting my lips, memories came pouring in. Memories that I had stuffed down and held down for dear life. Who would want me if they knew? Who would believe me? I don't remember much of the 5-hour drive home, except tears, a shaking body, a painful bleeding throat, and ANGER.

In that moment, I began to fully realize, the truth I had only partially accepted. Part of the sexual abuse as a child involved oral sex and

158

being ejaculated on. I knew it before, but my soul did not accept it, but now there was no hiding from it. It stood at the back of my throat like a great bloody warrior fighting its way out.

To this day, it is a trigger for me. Men tend to think it's so sexy and that every woman should want to perform oral sex for them. For me, it's painful, internally painful because of anger, hurt, disbelief, and damage physical damage first in childhood, then as an adult.

That event was the beginning to healing, but only the beginning. The risky behavior, the seeking attention in all the wrong places, and blindly trusting the untrustworthy continued for many more years until I could finally find a way to begin loving myself.

It was another 10 years before another piece of validation for that story came to my life and solidified it in my memory. Pappa was gone by then. There was no one left to save me, to hear me, to validate, and believe me.

I had been having some pain in my groin. Sharp deep pain that made it hard to walk and to lift my leg.

Once again, I was set back, back to that time and memory. Even though Pappa had told me the story, even though I was forced to recognize it through violent rape as an adult, part of me just could not completely absorb it.

I sought the help of an orthopedic doctor, as I was taking fists full of NSAIDS daily, multiple times a day to cope with the nagging pain that would keep me up at night. X-rays were ordered immediately which showed my right hip to be nearly completely bone on bone, and the left one only marginally better. I was 45, and I was told that my hips were deteriorating far too early. The doctor said that normally this happened at this age due to some kind of childhood trauma.

After the imaging consult, memories came flooding back of how my

LIFTED UP

hip would "pop" when I was a young girl and how I thought it was funny and would make it pop as I walked because my friend's hips could not do that. I felt special because of it!

Driving home I felt numb as if I was in some movie that I could not get out of. I fought so hard to not fully accept this story. Part of me accepted it, could recite the story, but there was still a little girl inside who was terrified and could not bear to look at it. Rage started to build in me because of what happened and because it had been hidden. Rage because if I spoke up I would be made to look like I was a lunatic and a liar. Rage because Pappa was gone and could not wipe away my tears anymore.

It was not the first time that I had received medical evidence of some childhood injury. Injury that I had been previously told was all in my head.

This story is not hard for me anymore. It is what it is. I understand that there are so many others who have been through similar or worse. Others who have not yet found a way to heal. Others still stuck in the cycle of risky sexual behavior seeking validation.

The only part that is difficult now is in the knowing that it will cause pain for those who still have not come to terms with the reality that I do remember, and my body does also.

I will not stop talking about it. I will not hide from it. Not for my validation, but for the hope that it helps another heal, helps another find some commonality, some inspiration that allows them to find hope within themselves to step out and become more, through and with the pain of abuse.

I am not alone. You are not alone.

CHAPTER 15

DESIGNING LIFE

"Miracles happen to those who believe in them."
Bernard Berenson

The keyboarding company we worked for began downsizing. Facing the possibility of being unemployed, I applied at a new company opening across the parking lot, a skiwear manufacturing facility for Serac.

Training began, and I hit the floor running. It was piecework, and my wage would depend on how much work I did. PERFECT! I could do this. For the longest time, I was the highest output piecework seamstress in the factory.

Learning quickly, I was promoted to lead. Repairing small issues on the many machines came naturally. Once taught about production efficiency, I utilized it to become the highest paid seamstress. It was not enough. I wanted to do more. I learned as many aspects of the factory as I could.

Standing with a stopwatch and clipboard in hand, I worked with the new seamstresses, observing, teaching, and streamlining their processes. Production engineering came naturally. Numbers, efficiency, and putting puzzles together were perfect for me.

LIFTED UP

Even that was not enough. I wanted more. I began working with the cut table, and I made trips to the main office to observe the designer and patternmakers at work. Piece by piece, the skills I would need to become a designer began to come together.

Managers at the factory changed. The man who was running it when I hired on had been let go. He was replaced with an aggressive young woman.

Curly hair, big eyes, and a bust that she loved to show off, she despised any woman who took attention from her. Advances were made toward most any of the men in the factory. Affairs between her and younger under age men began, which she only weakly tried to hide.

The workplace became increasingly volatile and corrupt. My home life was eroding quickly. Threats to leave would be followed by roses, apologies, and promises to change. The promises only lasted a week or two or until he thought I had forgotten.

Turtle Mountain Skiwear was formulated. The worst name ever for a skiwear company, it was my attempt to honor my heritage.

It was springtime in Seattle, and excitement filled the air. It felt fresh and new. The city made me smile, with its hustle and bustle and the change in attire and attitude from North Idaho. I felt like I belonged, and yet still felt like an outsider looking in. Somehow, I had managed to garner a booth at one of the clothing district trade shows presenting the few ski jackets I had designed and sampled up.

Nerves racing through my skin like rampant electrical bursts, the booth was set up and ready to go. As trade shows go, there were busy points and slow points. The slow points drug on unbearably. Still I managed to garner a contract and order for Mt. Spokane Ski patrol.

During the slow points, a sign would be posted "Be Right Back", and I would head to the restrooms taking advantage of the time to cruise by other booths and see what else and who else was out there.

MISHA FAYANT

A few aisles over from my booth, I found a young, well dressed, and charismatic Italian salesman. My heart skipped a beat when I sauntered by him, our eyes meeting. I may have tripped a little in my form fitting dress and stiletto heels.

It had been so long since anyone looked at me in that way. Not a creepy way, but a very smooth, sparkling energy that coursed through the air around him.

My marriage at home was all but barren. My husband too drunk to acknowledge me, except for his breakfast, lunch, or dinner orders.

I knew immediately that I was in trouble, giggling like a little girl as I walked away, doing my best to walk with grace. His eyes followed. Afternoon came, and it was his turn. He came by my booth. Tall, lean, and oozing confidence, he strutted straight toward me and introduced himself. The touch of his hand as he took mine made my knees buckle. It would be the beginning of a yearlong affair.

The newfound confidence I garnered from his attentions gave me enough courage to look for a new and different path in life.

Running away was something I had gotten good at. I excused it as being nomadic by blood. Regardless, I accepted an offer to come run the floor of a small sewing factory in Wyoming. Soon after arriving, the situation changed, and I was hired on as the designer.

I left my husband in Idaho. I could not take any more of the dysfunction, control, abuse, and alcoholism. The handsome salesman came to visit several times. He made me feel special, seen, whole, and loved. Distance and circumstance eventually dissolved the affair.

Living in Wyoming, my shell began to break apart a little. I held my head a little higher and had a spring in my step that had not been there for years. My confidence began growing as I stepped out working as a designer and engineer.

Trade shows in Las Vegas and Reno provided the adventures I needed. My trampled ego received bolstering, being away from my husband and Mom. I was seen and appreciated for the work I was doing.

In my mind, my marriage was all but over. I wanted to save money to file for divorce, but I spent far too much time enjoying my new life. Calls from my husband went unanswered. I could not stomach him. Tired of the game of apology only to return to old ways, I did not want to talk with him at all.

Male dancers prancing around in next to nothing invaded the old west saloon for a night. Every "good" LDS woman in town came out for the show. A male dancer caught my eye, and we began a relationship. I would travel to Salt Lake City on weekends to visit him.

By now, all the signs of drugs were apparent to me though I still knew little about them. Being more comfortable with our relationship, he never did them in front of me, but would lock himself in the bathroom for long periods of time. I could not go back to that kind of lifestyle. Handsome as he was, I packed my things while he was in the bathroom and left, never to return.

There was pressure from the ladies I worked with about taking my husband back. Failing to get through to me via phone, he began sending cards attempting to win me back.

One day, I was interrupted while running to and fro, managing the sewing floor, and progress of samples for the new line. The receptionist told me I had an important call that could not wait. She had tricked me! It was my husband, and now I was cornered. A conversation that was needed but that I did not want to have came rushing through the few moments on the phone.

MISHA FAYANT

If I agreed to allow him to come to Wyoming, he had to agree to stop smoking, stop the drinking, spend time with me, and pay attention to my needs. He quickly agreed.

Within a month he had arranged for Pappa to take our house by taking over payments, packed, and moved to Wyoming to patch up our relationship. The promises he made lasted only a few weeks. Drinking and eventually smoking weed appeared as if it had never left our life.

Our physical life was no different than before. It was rare!

Months had passed since his arrival. I kept a calendar of our sexual encounters. I was angry! It was tangible proof that his drinking was impeding our relationship. (That's what I told myself anyway.)

I made a trip across the border to a larger city in Idaho for shopping. Stomach pains and nausea made the trip almost unbearable. I called my best friend back in Wyoming confused and concerned that my female issues had come back. Giggling, she encouraged me to buy a pregnancy test.

What? NO! I pulled out my calendar and told her that in 3 months' time we had only been intimate 1 time. 1 time in 3 months!

Morning arrived, and I took the test. I stood in the bathroom looking for the telltale lines, sure that it would come out negative. I was positive the efforts were futile. There was no way I could be pregnant!

My heart stopped. I stood trying to refocus. How could it be positive? Reality sank in and with it joy, mediated by shock. It did not matter how. I was pregnant. After all this time, I would have a baby!

A doctor's visit confirmed the news, and the due date was set. I smiled and argued over the due date. I had a calendar remember! The date set was right in the middle of the "no sex" time period.

LIFTED UP

Thinking back later, I realized what had occurred during that time period that the doctor gave me as the time of conception. Pappa had visited. He, his wife, my husband and I all hiked up to a fresh water geyser that came straight out of the rock mountain face to create an ice-cold pool and waterfalls running down to a stream that meandered down the mountain.

The Native Americans from the region claimed it had healing powers and carried the energy of Mother Earth and creation from deep within. It was rumored that they came here in days past to cleanse and heal.

I wore clear quartz crystal, which hung from my neck as I climbed up the rocks toward the geyser. Everyone else stood below watching. Halfway up the trail, the geyser began gushing. Torrents of frigid water came rushing down toward me. Moving from the path to the rocks to avoid the flow, I heard terrified shrieks below me.

I was intent. I had a mission. I was there to pray for a child. Nothing was going to keep me from getting to the top to cleanse in the pool and pray.

"Miracles occur naturally as expressions of love. The real miracle is the love that inspires them. In this sense everything that comes from love is a miracle."
Marianne Williamson

Clinging to the rocks, now slippery with mineral waters, I slowly and carefully made my way up. Reaching the top just after the geyser finished spouting, my fingers, toes, and legs were numb from the cold. Teeth chattering, I remained focused on my goal.

MISHA FAYANT

All those trips to the doctor in Sandpoint had resulted in me being told the odds were I would not ever bear a child. I could not accept that answer. Willing to do whatever I could to become a mother, I now stood before the pool.

It was so cold! I could barely breathe just putting a foot in the water. Both feet back on the rocks outside the pool, I gathered all my intent, took a deep breath, and sank into the pool to pray.

Chattering, shivering, and quaking, I held my crystal, and prayed for healing and to be blessed with a child of my own. I sat praying for 10, 15, 20 minutes in that water, until tears were streaming down my face from the pain of the cold. Finally, I had felt it was time, and I stepped up out of the pool to make my way back down the rocks.

A bright proud smile, a nervous pacing woman, and an impatient, grumping husband all waited for me below. A peace had fallen over me climbing back down to my family waiting below.

Could it be? Was my prayer answered in that pool on that day? I have always said jokingly that my beautiful butterfly daughter was an immaculate conception. As it turns out, she would be born according to that timeline.

Back to work. Running the sewing floor became an embarrassing challenge. Morning sickness took over with a fury. I could not keep food down, not crackers or any of the wonderful suggestions I was given. The one trick that worked was to slowly suck on a spoonful of peanut butter. Going too fast would mean a trip to the ladies' room.

I'm not a quiet woman when I'm puking. The ladies' room also happened to be a simple box room built right into the middle of the production floor. Every time I was sick, it was painfully heard by anyone working nearby.

The company was growing, and with it came typical growing pains. Management fought, and we struggled to keep qualified seamstresses on board.

LIFTED UP

Outsourced manufacturing was sought out. I traveled in search of a facility to pick up our larger lines and relieve some load. The small factory had been outgrown by the growth in demand for our new designs.

A feeling of pride swept over me. I had been integral in that growth. My designs were being ordered in larger numbers, and it meant major shifts in the way we ordered textiles and handled production. Tensions ran high as the little company and its leaders struggled to keep up with the growth they had hoped for.

The pregnancy I had prayed for was fraught with challenges. My blood sugars spiked, and the placenta did not want to move out of the way. Sickness overtook my every day, as I struggled to keep up with the rapidly growing business, and I still had to deal with my drunken husband.

My feet and hands were so swollen, they were unrecognizable as my own. I could not wear normal shoes. I made a trip to Jackson Hole to see the doctor. Immediately, I was put on bedrest along with sitz baths in the hospital.

The longest needle I had ever seen was brought into my room in preparation for a test to pull amniotic fluid from my belly. Panic nearly overwhelmed me at the thought of that needle being pushed into my bulging mid-section. What searing, stabbing pain! I joke that my toe prints are still embedded in the footboard of that hospital bed as they clenched and hung on for dear life during the procedure.

My organs were failing, and the baby was failing. A decision to induce labor was made. There were rounds of nurse's hands rubbing gel on my cervix, and a dripline inserted into my arm delivering more medicine to make the contractions start.

After two days of contractions and a birth canal that felt on fire every time it was touched (It was later discovered I was allergic to the gel), both my energy and hope were fading. The contractions felt like I was being slammed against a wall then dropped to the floor every 3 minutes. I had refused a spinal, as I wanted the childbirth to be as drug free as possible.

Standing over the bed that held my sweating body, my husband and the doctor discussed the next steps.

I lay watching the monitor, riding the wild bull that was my contractions, and hearing their voices muffled through my pain. When I could catch my breath, I realized they were talking about taking the baby out via C-section. Finally, unable to cope with the pain any longer, I grabbed the doctor by the collar and screamed for him to take the "fucking drip" out of my arm. If I was not having a natural childbirth, I did not need more contractions!

My doctor and husband gave me a shocked look before rushing about to have the nurses remove the lines from my arm.

An emergency C-section finally brought my baby girl to my arms, and I rested in joy and peace.

Still having violent contractions, the anesthesiologist had struggled to administer the spinal block needed to allow me to be awake during the birth. With nurses holding my head to my knees through the contractions, he finally was able to find the spot he needed.

From that day forward, I have lived with back pain and sciatica down my right leg, causing weakness, burning, and pain that has worsened over time to inhibit even walking.

A few days later, our new little family made its way down the winding mountain road to our home. She was so tiny! Barely 5 pounds, we dressed her in "cabbage patch" doll clothes. Once home, she was diagnosed with severe jaundice and laid in the sun all day to help her turn around.

With the birth of this precious baby, my priorities changed drastically to thoughts of home and family. Wanting to provide her with accessibility to her grandparents and wanting to not be around the chaos of the skiwear industry (which was riddled with drug use) any longer, we chose to move back home to Idaho.

Pappa offered to give us our house back to have us home.

"It's not only moving that creates new starting points. Sometimes all it takes is a subtle shift in perspective, an opening of the mind, an intentional pause and reset, or a new route to start to see new options and new possibilities."
Kristin Armstrong

CHAPTER 16

RECLAIMING LIFE

*"You don't choose your family. They are God's gift
to you, as you are to them."*
Desmond Tutu

Car loaded to the gills, truck following behind, the long drive to North Idaho was filled with thoughts of returning home. I only had thoughts of allowing my baby to be around her family, as family had been so important to me as a child.

Through all the mishaps and pain, my extended family had given me so much joy. The visits to Mom's sister, Aunt Marylin's house—her matter of fact approach that was tempered with a soft soul—gave me respite from my own life and hope for something a little different. My Aunts all seemed so exotic to me in their own way. The cousins I gained through them felt like storybook characters that I would watch in awe and amazement.

Gatherings in Kalispell at Grandma's house or one of my Auntie's houses gave way to an alternate world and reality. Barbeques and family dinners spun around me like a thousand swarming butterflies. My heart smiled those days, and my head filled with wonder. I wanted my daughter to have those feelings and opportunities for love, growth, and happiness.

LIFTED UP

As flawed and broken as my life was, I wanted her to know and have time with her grandparents and as much of the family as she could. She was my parents' first grandchild. I saw a love and engagement with her from Mom that I only wished I had ever had. Pappa, well, he took her as his own personal butterfly, took pride and joy in all that she was, did, and could be.

The hole in my heart from those dark days growing up and the nightmares I endured made me want her to never experience that. I had hope that her little life would be different and better with far less pain. I focused on giving her all the opportunity I could for love from family. She was and has always been tender to Mom's heart. The plan must have worked.

Much of my life was spent in those reflective moments, hours, and days. Life itself was like walking in a dream, where I was there but strangely detached, as if watching from the viewpoint of a ghost halfway on her journey to the afterlife. Looking back, I realize how much my psyche attempted to shield me from the pain and sorrow that filled my heart and soul.

Then back to reality. Somehow the hours' long drive home had passed. The boxy little blue and white house my husband and I built stood in the field that was once a horse pasture with Pappa's truck standing as sentry. Sun shining and hot, the house shone like a bright blue earth stone in my mind.

The house inside was dingy from the smoke resin that covered the walls, floors, and ceiling. I spent hours and days scrubbing every surface attempting to clean the yellow tar and its accompanying stench from the walls to no avail. Still it was home, and we settled in. The lone bedroom downstairs that was once our bedroom now became the nursery. Upstairs, we lodged our furniture in the largest room.

The second floor had been built using lumber from an old cabin down by the river. We could use any materials from the old cabin if we tore the whole thing down and cleared it away. The land had been worth more without the structure than it was with it. It was waterfront property, and our little town was a last frontier of available, buildable lots.

Months had been spent tearing that little structure down, layer by layer, reclaiming anything we could possibly use. During that tear down, the years, layers, and lives of the house became clear. It had started out as a one-room log cabin over a hundred years earlier. Different inhabitants had added over decades one room at a time, until it became a jumbled mish mash home.

Tossing and turning restlessly, sleep never came easy in that room. Opening my eyes almost always meant the odd and unsettling vision of multiple people standing around the bed, clamoring for my attention.

Gasping in fright, I pulled blankets over my head as if to shield me from their presence. Was I going crazy? Had the years of trauma eroded my mind that much? Peeking out from under the blankets, the scene had not changed. They were still there. Then came the voices.

Once I acknowledged that I heard one, they began coming in vying for attention like a bunch of roadies at a concert. The sound was deafening at times. Inevitably I would look to my sleeping husband to see if he had seen or heard anything. Nope! He was sleeping soundly.

Night after night, a baby would be heard screaming and crying. Heart racing and half asleep, I would clamor down the stairs to my daughter's room, where she lay in peace. Sitting in the dark, I would watch her, waiting for any small indication that she had made the noises I heard.

That confirmation would never come. The screams continued, though not from her. Pain in my chest from the beating of my heart, and numbness in my head from confusion, lack of sleep, and self-doubt, continued to play on my sanity.

Back under the covers I would go pleading to be left alone and allowed to sleep. Sleep was no relief. It only magnified the things I saw and heard surrounding my bed. The cracks in my mind were shattering like great chunks falling from an iceberg. Even I doubted my sanity. The tattered aura that should protect and keep me was like a magnet for dysfunction, both on this plane and the spirit plane.

"Our feet are planted in the real world,
but we dance with angels and ghosts."
John Cameron Mitchell

Holding the visions and fears inside, I worried about the reaction from my husband if he ever knew. One day while playing in my room, my little girl asked, "Mommy? Do you hear that? Can't you hear that baby crying?"

Unsure of whether to feel fear or relief, I grabbed her and looked into her eyes asking, "What did you say?"

She then told me of the baby that lived in the room as I sat mouth gaping. More curious than scared, I sought out the help of one of my spiritual teachers who helped me understand what was happening and why. Methods to cope and lessen the instances and disturbances were given to my relief.

Deep cleansing breath! I was not crazy, just so scarred and weak that I was being preyed upon by those wanting and or needing to be heard. We worked on controlling the instances for myself and for my little girl. By now, I was more convinced than ever that she was/is an angel incarnate on earth.

Drunken rage faced me nightly, and I could no longer bear sleeping in that room with voices and ghosts and an increasingly angry husband. I spent most nights sleeping on the floor next to the toddler bed that held my baby girl. Holding her hand staring at her sleeping little face infused some peace into my soul. Her room felt like a hideout and a sanctuary.

A calendar was my outlet for keeping sanity. It provided tangible proof of the happenings in the house. Drinking, sex, my monthly cycle, bills due, appointments made, marks were made for anything and everything that could be scheduled or tracked.

My cycle had always been irregular, so I did not even notice that my period had not come for months. The next trip to town meant a visit to the pharmacy to find a pregnancy test. Once again, the confusion built. How could I be?

Tracking back to my last period, it began after I had begun sleeping on the floor next to my baby girl. No marks had been made for intimate encounters for a very long time. Mostly because he was often too drunk to care, and I could not stomach his touch.

Early in the dark of the not yet risen sun, holding a small strip between my legs, the pressure of my first morning urine hit the tip. Lying on the counter, I watched as the urine soaked up the indicator making the plain white turn to colored line. Double checking the product box, I stood staring, back and forth. Once again, the resounding thought was "How?" A little laugh escaped my lips, and I proclaimed internally—another immaculate conception. I must be the only "barren" woman with little or no sexual contact with her husband to have conceived twice during a "drought".

A doctor's visit confirmed that his conception had been right smack in the middle of the weeks spent sleeping on the floor. It no longer mattered. I was being given a gift. A second child! I had been researching adoption, but we did not ever get along long enough or have enough financial stability to allow me to take it seriously.

The gift was given and had been received. I was going to have another child. This pregnancy went much easier. Morning sickness was all but nonexistent. I found happiness in the prospect of another baby to love. Hugs, attention, and love had been focused on my little girl because it was non-existent from my husband. I would now have another outlet for the love I wanted and needed to give.

"The gain is not the having of children;
it is the discovery of love and how to be loving."
Polly Berrien Berends

Premonitions of an impending divorce, coupled with my own commitment to lessen the load of human population on Mother Earth, drove me to plan for a tubal ligation after the birth of this child. Either the relationship would repair and be tolerable, or I would make my exit. If it repaired, then I would push to adopt, and give an unwanted child a home and a parent who would love them. I never got that chance.

Narcissism was not a word I knew but was well acquainted with. Fights within the marriage continued and worsened, no matter how committed I attempted to be. No matter how many times I tried to straighten up and be a good wife. "If I just do more, clean more, cook better, or spend less, he will not be so unbearable. Maybe he will love me again."

Mom had convinced me to open a bridal and floral shop in Sandpoint. We found a location right on one of the main shopping streets downtown. An old western wear shop with large custom cases built into the walls, glass and wood doors that swung open to expose the previously protected goods within.

It was perfect! Perfect for holding the heavy white dresses of a bridal store, perfect for protecting them from dirty, probing hands. We set up shop, installing the floral shop in the back room. Coolers were brought in along with a large surface worktable. My office was inserted into one of the balconies overlooking the sales floor. The other balcony held storage and a small stock of in-house tuxedo rentals.

Spending as much time as I could away from home, the little shop in Sandpoint gave me escape. The enterprise was doomed from the start. The stock that I had been promised to help fill the shop and get a start was all outdated dresses from a few years prior that had not been sold in Montana. The Sandpoint crowd, being a bit more progressive, noticed right away and began complaining. New dresses were brought in. The bills mounted.

Calls came in every day of things needed for home. Items were expected to be paid for out of the cash register of the fledgling business. Money that should have been paying startup costs was going directly into the household. Soon enough, the business imploded under the weight of demands.

I had only received unhealthy financial modeling from my childhood. Food and spending were my emotional coping mechanisms. Following that lead, I ate and spent. He pulled money from the business for household needs. Angry that I was building something outside of him and that I spent so much time outside of the house, he demanded restitution.

That pregnancy kept my hopes up. The child growing inside me and the one already at my feet helped me focus on good things to come.

Stress from all corners crashed in on me during those last days of my pregnancy. My husband wanted it to be over. There was too much attention going everywhere but him and home. Mom was watching intently, waiting for this new child to arrive. Friends constantly asking about the baby, the business needing me and me wanting the baby out. The weight of it all was so heavy!

False labor hit multiple times. The half hour trek to town was made more than once only to have the contractions stop once inside the hospital room. I began running stairs to encourage the baby to drop and come out. I consumed castor oil hoping for the contractions to

LIFTED UP

hold. (I have not been able to keep castor oil in the house since. It was horrible!) Sit-ups, long drives, and jumping jacks—nothing helped.

Sitting on the end of the exam table in the hospital, contractions had finally taken hold. Excitement mixed with disappointment muddled my head. Husband had been exasperated and frustrated, which led him to insist I drive myself to the hospital. He needed to go to work. Now the doctor's voice came seeping through the clouds of thought as his face pushed directly in front of me. As it focused in to the landscape of my mind I could make out his question. "Where is your husband, Mrs. Waits?"

I could hear my voice, feel my mouth moving, but I was so focused on holding back tears; tears from feeling abandoned yet again in life. Memories of the last time I was in the hospital undergoing the laparoscopy. It was the same thing. I brought myself in. I spent the day alone. I had to call pleading for him to come get me because the hospital would not release me without someone there.

My voice sounded so distant and foreign, "He's at work. He did not want to take time off to be here." The coping mechanisms had kicked in. A spiritual shroud within that shielded me from things I could not bear.

Coaxing me into full attention, the doctor began to explain that I was indeed in labor. However, I was so stressed, tense, and so tired, my cervix was not dilating. I needed to relax. But how?

Morphine was being offered. NO! I would not drug my unborn child. The doctor took my hand gently but firmly and explained either I could take the morphine, rest for a few hours, and hopefully let the cervix dilate so the child could be born, or continue as I was.

Continuing would likely mean days of labor. Not taking the morphine, as he explained it, would likely put my unborn child at more risk due to the obvious stress I was under. My cervix may tear, and I may end up with a second C-section. All the options he was laying out before me would put my baby in as much or more danger than me taking a dose of morphine.

178

MISHA FAYANT

Struggling with the decision and exhausted from the labor and the prior week's false alarms, I vacillated. Becoming a bit agitated (rightfully so), he finally demanded a decision. I could not believe the words that came out of my mouth. I would take the morphine. I was already too tired to hold my head up, and I would be no good to my baby in this state.

Holding a tray, the nurse appeared, prepping me for the injection. Tears flowing, I watched her insert the needle into my arm, as I prayed for my baby's safety. They moved me to a quiet room where everything began to blur and then go black. Hours later, the room began to spin into view again, a canvas of grey and soft edges coming slowly into focus.

Pushing the call button, I announced that I was awake and ready to go! The nurse arrived, checked my cervix, and now only a few hours later I was ready to begin the path to delivery. Along with the contractions, I had low back pain so intense it felt as if my spine was being severed.

Hot water! My room had a shower, and I spent most of the afternoon in it, hot soothing water flowing down my back.

Friends came. Once again, the question of the day—where was my husband? His best friend and a manager at the mill where he worked was miffed at the thought he was not here. I explained we had called, and he had refused to come. The best friend called work told them to find him, and tell him to get his ass to the hospital.

Back in the shower I went. As evening approached, Husband finally by my side (he finished his shift), the pains increased dramatically. Stepping out of the shower I felt as if I had to poop, and so I sat on the toilet straining and pushing. Like a book to the back of my head I could hear Mom's voice, "Having a baby feels like having to take the biggest poop of your life." I sat up straight. Excited! Could it be? Was this it?

Waddling out to the room where everyone gathered, chatting and waiting, I exclaimed, "The baby is coming!" Sure enough, he was crowning and pushing his way out. This was a new experience. I still refused a spinal or any drugs, but the contractions were nothing at all like those that attempted to bring my daughter into the world. Push after push, I bore down until I heard a snap! (I had broken my already fragile tailbone pushing). Not long after, my baby boy was in my arms.

What is his name? The necessary paperwork was being filled out. "Damon Louis Waits," we exclaimed. As the nurse was writing, I could see Mom out of the corner of my eye. She had been present for the whole birth. In fact, she demanded that my 13-year-old sister be there to witness the pain of childbirth as some kind of mental birth control. Without a word, she stormed out of the birthing room.

Pappa's name was Louis. Hearing his name, she could not bear to look at this child. Her demeanor went from love of her new grandchild to one of disgust. She went home and busied herself cleaning my house and preparing for me to come home with the baby. As soon as we arrived, she left and headed back to Montana.

This set the stage for my son's relationship with her. Unwittingly, I had set him up for failure with her. She never treated him the same as my daughter. He could feel it and sense it. It would eventually cause the demise of their relationship.

The Wedding shop could not bear the weight of the financial burden or my absence from its daily workings and was soon out of business.

The kids filled my life with love, and my attention was firmly directed away from my husband. I did not care! He had not paid me attention for years. In my mind, he deserved to be lonely and set aside. I had my kids now, and he was not the center of my universe or in control of my happiness.

Our relationship continued to erode. His drinking worsened. I gauged my activities with the kids based on when he would be home. Weekends meant getting them up early and getting out of the house before the bear woke and swung his claws at us. I set up a sewing room in the basement. I took up quilting and began prolifically creating. It was my safe space, my respite from his presence.

MISHA FAYANT

Days I could no longer see from the tears that drowned my eyes, I escaped to the basement. Days my heart could bear no more degradation, I would sew with a fervor. Dysfunction at its finest manifested in every crevice of my life. That basement collected scraps and materials in mountains of mess and debris, mirroring the depths of despair in my soul.

I had begun retreating from life. So many days of being told how stupid, unworthy, and unattractive I was had compounded into wounds that refused to heal. How did I end up here? In my mind, I must be as disgusting as Mom and he had said. Both had declared it so many times I could not see me without the weight of those words. The story of being not enough deepened in my being and the invisibility cloak tightened around me, suffocating me.

Depression crept in, sticking its dirty foot in every room in my heart. Soon thoughts of ending my life filled my head. The voice that said I was not needed, not loved, and not enough screamed louder and louder as I shrunk from existence. Those days in the basement, turned into days crying as I created. The basement hideout buried me away from sight.

My baby sister was all grown up now and engaged to be married. Mom commissioned me to make a wedding quilt for her. The result was the purchase of a quilting machine, one that took up half the width of the basement.

Patches were sent to family and friends to embroider. I was given material and told she liked quilts with different designs for each block and so my work began. I designed a quilt planning out a different design for each one utilizing common materials throughout. The centerpiece of the quilt was a large sculpted angel with long flowing red hair. This was an angel I drew, designed, and carefully pieced into a fabric piece of art.

Making this quilt was cathartic, and it helped me hold on. Creating and working on an angel gave space for me to feel special and needed. It was a culmination of hundreds of hours, but the outcome was amazing. It was like a painting of fabric surrounded by patchwork. I felt pride. What an odd feeling, but such a beautiful feeling. Pride in something I had done, not pride in my children or loved ones. Pride for myself.

Through all the ups and downs of those married years, I had begun to hang out with a new crowd---a group of healers, empaths, and spiritually based men and women in North Idaho. Learning came in at a rapid pace. Spiritual fairs were taken in as often as possible. Books about anything spiritual were devoured as I searched for a way to heal my heart and soul.

"Most women I know are priestesses and healers... We are, all of us, sisters of a mysterious order."
Marianne Williamson

Time and again, I was told that I was meant for far more than I realized. One healer my Pappa introduced me to in Spokane began to piece things together and give me some direction and hope. One of the symbols she told me that was associated with me was that of a raven, because it could go into the darkness that would consume others and come out intact and with a needed message or lesson.

That was when I slowly began to change how I viewed the events in my life. It was slow changing the stories, healing the wounds, and finding ground solid enough to stand on without toppling over spiritually. I still had much to learn, but the lessons had begun.

Slowly, I developed the tools to slow and stop the nightmares and regulate the souls demanding my attention. The pieces of my family started to make sense and fall into place giving me understanding and allowing me to accept each person for their role no matter how damning it seemed.

MISHA FAYANT

Visions had come and gone all my life, and I was used to watching them unfold and come true. I also understood that physical clues manifesting throughout my body were indicators of the world around me. The back of my head would burn and throb in unbearable pain when I was around extremely negative people, even if unknowingly just walking by them in a store or passing on the street.

Goosebumps started being understood as indicators of "truth" being spoken or unfolding. I felt so new and awestruck by the world unfolding before me. The acceptance by others of the gifts that Mom had so long told me were evil, gifts that I had learned not to speak about in the presence of others.

Pappa's mom was institutionalized for being crazy for these same gifts. I learned to hide them and be wary of them. Now all that began to fall away as I learned what "gifts" they truly were and began to sort through understanding them.

Bodies filled the small living room of my home as an esteemed healer/teacher from Canada came in. Arranging for her to come teach a weekend workshop would prove to change my life forever. I was still just learning and still unsure of all these things and wary of teachings that contradicted the teachings of the Lutheran and Nazarene churches I had grown up in.

Colors dimly began to show up around the head of my friend as I squinted practicing seeing auras. I had seen them before but did not understand. Now I was being trained to see and understand them, along with my friends. One by one, we worked through gifts and tools as taught by my Canadian guest. I began to feel like a seed that was bursting through the soil to grow and expand, opening into a full flower reaching for the sun.

Reincarnation. Here we go! I sat quietly as I watched the group one by one being guided through "past lives" and learning to help their workshop buddy through the regression. My eyes would roll as I heard the things they were saying, knowing in my soul that it was not real. Sure, that they were just making shit up, I was detached and had no real interest in being part of It all.

183

LIFTED UP

The last pair—it was my turn, and I did not really want to go. Hesitantly, I laid back and closed my eyes listening to the words being told to me. Pictures began coming in from centuries ago that I could not explain. Moving forward through stories, I still was not sure how much weight I gave any of it. I would explain it as an overactive imagination.

Images came in of being in a village. The dwellings were dome shaped. I recognized those as being the typical structure of my native ancestors. Buckskin draped over me, there was a little girl, my daughter and a small boy, my son. The story seemed to unfold centered around him. Cooking on an open pit fire, my children playing nearby, I was startled by shouting and screaming.

Men in black coats on horseback came riding into the camp along with men dressed differently. Fighting ensued and children were abducted, screaming and reaching for their mothers. (I don't know where the men were). The little boy fought, crying and reaching for me, he hit the man holding him, and then bit him.

Startled, the man jumped and dropped my son whose head landed on a rock. Another man scooped him up and took him away. Chasing after them, crying and pleading for my children. The man who took my son was recognized in this lifetime as my older brother.

The whole scene was disturbing. Still I fought believing any of it could be true. Watching my son being taken from me was more than I could take, and I was brought to, just in time for me to run to the bathroom and throw myself in front to the toilet to puke violently between tears and gut-wrenching sobs that took my breath away.

My children and husband were not present for the workshop. The kids did not know of the story of my regression and its details. I filed it away as a farce, and I was just being emotional at the thought of my son being taken and harmed. I did not speak of it in the house and just tried to forget that portion of the weekend.

Pouring rain, accompanied by summer thunder booming and lightening crackling, lighting up the cloud laden evening sky entertained us. The kids and I loved sitting in the yard or on the porch watching the night sky. Rain often sent us to the porch to take refuge from the downpours. The scent, sound, and feel of rain has always been healing for me.

We sat on the porch until the sky turned black from the cloud cover and the thunder booms timed too close to the flash and crack of the lightning. Moving our little party inside, my son took my hand and said, "Momma, can I talk to you after Sissy goes to bed? I have a story to tell you."

He was always a serious child (he still is!). But the look on his face was so earnest and urgent, I could not deny him. When my daughter decided she was tired enough to go to bed, he followed me to my room to tell me his story. My mind raced. What could this little man have up his sleeve that was so important?

"Important encounters are planned by the souls long before the bodies see each other."
Paulo Coelho

Such a big man even at 4, he told me to lay down, then held my head. He said, "Momma, I have to tell you something, and I want you to just listen until I'm all done. It's important." His little hands stroked my hair as if to sooth me and tell me it would be okay.

He began by telling me the story I had seen in my past life regression, including how he fell and hit his head. Shocked, I moved to look into his eyes. He gently pushed my head back down, and said, "I know Momma, but what you don't know is what I need to tell you about." I settled back in and tried to calm myself and let this little man speak.

LIFTED UP

He painted a picture of his life after being taken. He was taken to a Catholic school where they taught him English, tried to get him to wear "civilized clothes", told him that they were doing all this for his own good. He fought as hard at the school as he had the day they took him. One day he was finally able to escape.

He told me he went back to the spot where we had made camp the day they took him, but we were gone. Years had passed. He then spent his time searching; following the pieces of information he could gather. Our small band was nomadic, and it took a few more years before he found us.

He leaned over me as tears streamed down my face, and quietly said, "It's okay, Momma, I found you. You were old, but I did not give up. We were together again. You can rest now, Momma. I found you."

By now, you would think I would be accustomed to things like this. This one though, it shook me. I had not told him that story, he had no way of knowing, and he had told it back to me almost exactly as I had seen it. How could this little 4-year-old boy know and understand any of this? Here he was comforting me and soothing me to tell me a story that needed completion.

That day changed everything. I questioned everything I knew and opened to a whole new world of possibilities. So much made sense now.

Whenever someone tried to take him from me as a child, he would cry and get a crushing headache. We had gone to Disneyland with Mom the year before. She had been more abrupt with him his whole life than she was with my daughter. At Disneyland, when he was only 3 years old, she expected him to keep up with us as we walked and would get angry when he wanted to ride in the stroller or took too long.

At one point, she grabbed him from me because he needed to use the restroom. He screamed and cried the whole time. He complained of a horrible headache and could do nothing else that day but cling to me, which angered her even more. She and I fought that day. I screamed at her. He was only 3!

Understanding the triggers for him, we began to work on releasing them and he eventually was able to be away from me without the headaches and panic.

CHAPTER 17

IT'S A FAMILY THING

'There is a universal, intelligent, life force that exists within everyone and everything. It resides within each one of us as a deep wisdom, an inner knowing. We can access this wonderful source of knowledge and wisdom through our intuition, an inner sense that tells us what feels right and true for us at any given moment.'
Shakti Gawain

My grandmother on my Pappa's side was very psychically gifted. She saw and foretold things others could not understand. There were periods of time when she was locked in mental hospitals because she scared people, especially the white people who did not understand our culture and thought that, surely, she was possessed. Nothing like this could come from God and must be blasphemy or the devil.

One account was of an uncle. She saw him working near a haystack, had seen him have a heart attack grasping at his chest, and he fell into the hay. There was something about a pitchfork; I don't remember if he fell on it or if it was just in his hand as he fell. Grandma, by all reports, went into a trance-like state screaming and crying as she watched it unfold. She was able to tell the relatives where he was and how they would find him. At her insistence, they rushed to his place to find him exactly as she described.

MISHA FAYANT

Mom also had the gift, but because of her religious upbringing she was told much like Pappa's mom that it was not a gift. She believed that it was a curse. I remember when an Aunt had been diagnosed with cancer and died within a few months. Mom had seen the death beforehand and felt guilt over it. When I asked her about it, she looked stern and said, "It is not a gift! It is a curse, and I wish to never see things again!" She then broke down sobbing in tears, laying in her bed wailing.

I had no idea how to console her. I was so intrigued by her gift and confused as to why she would deny it or think it a curse. After that incident, as far as I know, she shut down her gift by denying it. We only ever spoke of it again when I began seeing things at the home she moved to in Montana with her new husband.

I could see a man, feel his presence, and I heard things move. When I asked, she knew exactly what it was, and who it was.

One night while sleeping in a makeshift bed, in what used to be the back of a western wear store, he ran on the main floor of their home. I woke to see a man standing at the foot of my bed. I was terrified, frozen in fear and disbelief. I thought surely, I was losing my mind, until my daughter woke, sat up grabbing my hand and let out a blood curdling scream. "Who was that man?" she cried as she clung to my arm sobbing in fear.

Conversations with my mother and younger sister later confirmed that it was the uncle of my stepdad who had not transitioned on from the store and home. He had built it and the business that it had contained and so he rambled about in the store and basement for years.

There were many stories and instances of Grandma's gift, a gift that Father carried, a gift that was passed to me. I have always seen "ghosts", ancestors, spirits, and they have spoken to me. I have seen things that others could not explain how I knew.

LIFTED UP

It took years of learning and studying with medicine men and intuitives to learn to control it so that I was not so plagued by nightmares and sightings of unwanted guests.

Traveling across Montana that summer of PowWow, the kids and I stopped at Little Bighorn. It was amazing to be there and stand on the ground where so much history had been made, but we were not prepared for what would happen.

Walking the grounds, we saw scenes reenacted, scenes that only we could see. We saw the souls of many natives as we walked. At first it was intriguing. Soon it became disturbing and overwhelming. We had planned to stay the night, but all 3 decided we would rest better if we were not in a place with so much unrest.

That summer upon arriving in Devil's Lake, North Dakota, we found Pappa, living in a home directly across the street where he had lived as a young man. We all 3 were excited to see his sparkling blue eyes and mischievous grin.

We sat listening to stories of what he was doing that summer and the home he had lived in. We played games and visited with relatives all evening. Finally, when it was time for bed, the two kids and I crowded into a double-size bed in a back room. They were so excited they could barely sleep.

Just as we all were falling asleep, I had a vision. It was as if there were a hundred television screens flashing before my eyes 20 or so at a time. Visions of past, present, future, came zooming by rapid fire. I was not sure what it all meant. I still don't know what some of it was.

The next day, the kids and I drove up to the reservation where our tribe is from, and one-by-one, I started seeing places from those visions.

Those days visiting the reservation and family were filled with odd memories and feelings that could not be explained. At times, it felt as if I could hear my ancestors calling out to me, desperate to give me messages and information.

Pappa encouraged me to listen to the voices and visions. They had come and gone my whole life. To this day, there are things that just cannot be explained and things I have learned not to talk about. Unfortunately, it often had meant being called crazy or "not right in the head".

"It is through science that we prove,
but through intuition that we discover."
Henri Poincare

CHAPTER 18

FREEDOM THROUGH DIVORCE

"Every woman that finally figured out her worth, has picked up her suitcases of pride and boarded a flight to freedom, which landed in the valley of change."
Shannon L. Alder

Being out in public was painful for me. I had spent so much time accepting the words that were told to me about how unattractive I was, how no one wanted to see or hear from me that I believed it to my core. Even in the heat of summer I would wear jackets in an attempt to cover up what no one wanted to see. When strangers would give compliments, I would shrink away as if they had tossed acid on me.

I had put on a tremendous amount of weight. That weight shielded me and made sure that I was hidden beneath it, assuring that no one would look at me. My subconscious did a bang-up job of tasking my body with upholding the contract of that story I accepted for myself.

Spiritual growth meant I began gaining personal strength. The bouts of suicidal depression began to ease. The more self-confidence I gained, the more friends I made, and the more my husband felt threatened.

We had fight after torturous fight. Money was the one thing most important to him, above the kids and me. For the longest time, we had a traditional checking account. It caused so much anguish. All the money in the account was "his" to use at his discretion, but I had to ask for every penny spent or account for it.

Before the wedding shop was closed, we had taken a trip to Spokane one day to do some shopping. It was still customary and polite to wear pantyhose at the time. I picked out the cheapest pack that I could find, a pack of 10 for 5 or 6 dollars, and some underwear because mine were tattered with holes and the elastic waistbands coming off. He gathered hunting items, and his own personal things. Not one word was said about my items the entire time we shopped through that store.

Standing at the checkout counter unloading the cart, my nerves began kicking in. This was always the time conflict occurred. This day was no different, as the checkout belt neared the cashier, he began grabbing my items, shouting, "I'm not paying for this shit!" and throwing it back in the cart. The cashier stood face showing confusion and pity as he looked over at me. We left the store without my items as I was forbidden to purchase them.

Years of this went on, and we were splintering rapidly. I devised a logical plan in my mind. I had taken a job in Sandpoint at a manufacturing facility and had an income of my own. I opened my own checking account. Sitting down with him I laid out my plan. We took all the family bills and listed them out including amounts. I used paystubs to determine each of our income and the resulting percentage of income to the household. We then split the bills, I made about 40% of the income so we divided out 40% of the bills to my responsibility, and the other 60% were the bills he would take over and assume payment of.

Simple, fair I thought it was reasonable. The money we each had in excess of our required bills could be spent as we each pleased. For me, it meant books and other spiritual supplies and things for the kids and me. For him, it often meant alcohol and hunting equipment.

His booming, angry voice filled the air as books came flying across the living room. My purchases were tangible and static, his primarily ended up literally "pissed down the toilet". He began demanding that I pay more of the bills since I had so much money to waste on this "shit". To no avail, I tried to explain things and our agreement. Soon bills went unpaid, as he chose to buy alcohol instead.

Head down working on an order at the equestrian manufacturer, I was interrupted by the all too familiar sound of his angry voice. He had burst into work, holding the checkbook growling about an 8-dollar check that had "milk and bread" written in the memo line. Shaking the checkbook, headed straight for me yelling, "Milk and bread do not cost 8 dollars! Where did the rest of the fucking money go? Tell me! Tell me right now!"

Shock set in and I could not move, I felt like a stone figure sitting in that chair. Eyes filled with pity, shock, and dismay looked back at me from around the room. The owner came out from behind his desk telling him to take it outside. Shaking, I followed him out the door. PTSD settled in and I could not think.

I struggled to make sense of anything except the checkbook waving in front of my face and smacking across my shoulder accompanied by angry words that fell like stones on my head. I just wanted it to stop. How the heck did I remember what I bought weeks ago? I was not released until I could explain.

Returning to my station inside, still shaking, co-workers surrounded me with apologies and consolation. They knew of our troubles, but none believed it was as bad as I said. That day proved as more than some small evidence.

I was given slips of paper with contact numbers for agencies that dealt with spousal abuse with instructions to call someone right away. I think that some of them were more traumatized than even I was that day. Reality smacks heavy when you're in denial.

MISHA FAYANT

The reports to his family were that he could not pay the bills because of my spending. There were many family meetings in secret, discussing how to deal with his insolent wife.

His anger was escalating. The kids and I spent more time planning when to be home and when to be gone based on when he would be there, when he would wake up, or go to bed. It seemed like we walked on eggshells daily.

Drunken shouting came booming from the kitchen I walked in to see what the issue was. A cup came flying at my head narrowly missing me because I ducked, shattering on the wall behind me. Something was not put away where he wanted it, and so everything was being drug out and thrown.

This had been going on so long. I remember a time when we had a moment's peace, sitting in the dark, all watching a movie on tv. Thump, thump, thump, the noise brought terror to my soul. He hated random noises and became violent at the interruption of them. My son had inched too close to the entertainment center - one of those old ones that had a storage door on the side for VHS tapes. As children do, he was tapping it with his foot. I jumped up and quietly said "Don't do that, you're making Daddy angry", as I pulled he and his sister back further from the TV.

Sitting in our separate recliners, lost in the movie, I did not recognize the thumping when it began again. When it did register I was too late, he had beat me getting up. My son was turned upside down, head banging on the floor, leg in his dad's hands. Hands that clenched his little leg, twisting it and torqueing it while his dad screamed, "You were told to stop, I'm going to break your fucking leg!"

Quickly I moved to interject. Begging him to let go of my son, burning fear building in my gut that my son's leg would be snapped at any moment. Finally, he let go, dropping my son smack on his head. I scooped up my shaking and crying little boy, sitting down with him still crying, rocking, and trying to soothe him.

LIFTED UP

Profanity flooded over us. "Mamma's boy! Fucking little Mamma's boy. Stop your God damn crying little fucking Mamma's boy." Over and over it continued for at least 15 minutes longer. Anger seethed through me and in the back of my mind I knew I was nearing my end. Something had to change; we could not live like this anymore.

In quiet, preparations were made to mentally ready myself. It was a different time. In that North Idaho environment, I had seen many other women struggle to survive. Women who lived in their cars with their kids and all their belongings packed in around them. Kids going to school dirty and stinky picked on by their peers.

My head swam, struggling to find solid ground wherein I could make a decision. Stay and deal with the abuse or leave and end up living out of our car? Which scenario was more damning to the kids? What to do!? Friends all had a unified and resounding message. I had to get out.

Food still on the table, I sat quietly finishing my dinner as the kids went to the bathroom to clean up and brush their teeth after eating. Bickering followed by yelling, emanated from the open bathroom door. I looked up just in time to see them come walking out, my daughter cowering, head down (she looked like me) my son following, hitting her over the back and chastising her for something simple (he resembled his Dad).

In that moment, I realized that they were modeling the adults. In that moment I realized one simple fact. I was damning them to repeat our relationship. If I could not summon enough strength to save myself, I had to summon enough save my babies.

One of my friends was a psychologist. She had just recently counseled me on the effects of abuse on the kids. The one resounding message I carried with me was this. Kids will seek out in their adult partners, whatever, whomever mimic the role models in their lives when they turn 10. At 10 it is solidified, in younger years it can be changed. The message to me was firmly a case that I needed to get my kids out of this situation and provide them with something healthier even if it was a single parent household.

MISHA FAYANT

She had imparted to me the premise that little girls will seek out a man who models the behaviors and characteristics of the man in their life at the age of 10. Little boys will seek out a woman who modeled the mother figure in their life at that same age. If the male figure was selfish and abusive, that is what I was setting up for my daughter to find. I could not bear that thought. Nor could I bear the thought that my son would become his father and seek out a woman who would accept the abuse as I had been doing.

That day, that moment, something in me snapped. It was done I had to leave. In secret, I began looking for a home for the kids and me. It took some time to set it all up. Mom had already recognized the need and encouraged me to invest in a business that could support the kids and me. A second mortgage was taken out, we flew to California for training, and ordered product. Returning home, the search became finding a space that could house both the business and my kids. A double wide trailer situated between the small towns of Priest River, ID, and Newport, WA, seemed like a good place, allowing accessibility for clients from both towns, which were situated only a few miles apart.

Quietly, we set up the business and then one day while he was at work, I moved the kids and I out and into that trailer. I felt it was the only safe way to do it.

Mom had come to help and stayed to watch the kids, while I went back to the old house to confront him. He was in shock. After all the warnings I had given, he never took me seriously, secure in his hold over me. He went from crying, begging, and pleading me to stay to threats of killing himself.

"If you spend your time hoping someone will suffer the consequences for what they did to your heart, then you're allowing them to hurt you a second time in your mind."
Shannon L. Alder

LIFTED UP

Having dealt with enough and my heart being turned to stone where he was concerned I replied, "Please do! I'll get more from Social Security for the kids then I ever will from child support." Shock and dismay ran across his face, but then came the anger. The threats turned toward me, detailing how he was going to kill me and take the kids. I was not so cocky now! Quickly making my exit to my waiting car, I could feel him on my heels, feel his hands grasping for me as I left. I just had to open my mouth!

For 15 years, our pattern had been I would threaten to leave. He would apologize and promise to stop drinking to treat me better. A few days to a few weeks later, and then everything would return to the normal abusive relationship we had built. This time was no different. He poured on the charm coming to visit the kids and me. I did not deny him time with the kids, but I had no desire to return to him.

Fresh, new mattress! It had been a struggle, but it was the one thing I was determined to have—a bed he had never laid in. Visiting the kids one day, he apparently thought it was a good time to make advances toward me. I had stepped away to use the bathroom in my room. When I walked out, he laid sprawled across my bed, making suggestive motions and letting me know he had sent the kids to play.

My gut churned. "NO! Get off my bed," I heard the words come screaming out of my mouth, and I ran to the bed hitting him and pulling him off. He looked so confused by it all. He had been so sure of himself; he was not prepared for that reaction at all. Demanding he leave, I escorted him to the door.

Curves, the lady's fitness chain, was the beginning to me reclaiming my health and losing some weight. Once I gained some confidence, I purchased a membership at the gym in town, and I was there 5 days a week getting stronger on the outside to match what was building on the inside.

The kids both played basketball. Those games meant shared space with him. It was tolerable, but uncomfortable. He still was vacillating between charm and anger. Anger was increasingly becoming the go to emotion as it began sinking in that I was not coming back to him. At one particular game, as he and I sat on the stage edge overlooking the little guys running up and down the court, an argument ensued. My daughter perched right between us (strategically to keep separation between he and I).

I did not flinch or shy away like I had during our marriage. It frustrated him. I felt some power back in my being; "You will find it harder to hurt me now that I have been working out" I spewed at him. Anger, seething anger crossed his face as he paused a moment before turning to me to say, "You may be stronger than me now, but I still have a gun. I'll just come shoot your ass. That will take care of that. I won't have to worry about you ruining my life anymore."

Jaw dropped, I sat staring at him. Did he really just threaten to kill me right in front of my daughter? Yep, he sure did, and he meant it! The look in his eyes sent chills down my spine. He went on to tell me how he would do it. He would sneak onto the property and come right up the front deck that gave him access to my bedroom window. He detailed how he knew where my bed was placed and how easy it would be to just put the gun near the glass and shoot me as I slept, and then he would take the kids.

I made a report to the local police, but they did not take it seriously. At home, I rearranged everything. My mattress was leaned up against the window to block it. Doors were locked inside and out. Mine was the only room that had a locking door, so at night we would all pile into my room, sleeping on the floor inside the closet. Exterior doors and my bedroom door locked, the kids thought it was and adventure that we had built a fort. I did not have the heart to tell them Mommy was scared for her life.

LIFTED UP

Divorce papers were drafted. We had agreed to settle out of court. I had thought we had a chance of salvaging at least a little dignity out of our marriage. Delivering the papers to him, he had a change of heart. He was going to fight.

Pappa's birthday was only 2 days apart from my daughter, Minda's. They had always spent their birthdays together. There was no court order for visitation yet. We had just been working together to make things happen. Arrangements were made, to which he agreed, for me to take Minda to Central Washington to visit her grandpa for their birthdays.

It was now a year since I left him. I had begun dating a man from Virginia, a big stout football and track and field coach. He had made plans to come visit for the weekend. He was going to ask my Pappa for permission to marry me (as soon as the divorce was final). My soon-to-be ex-husband heard of his visit that weekend and decided he was not going to allow me to take the kids as had been planned.

Working as a bookkeeper for a local construction company, I was in charge of getting payments out for taxes. That week my boss had been difficult, delaying approval of the bills until the last minute. Checks were written and given to him mid-week. By Friday, he had still not signed them. Multiple calls were made informing him of the need for them to be signed and postmarked that day to avoid fees. The calls also reminded him that I needed to leave on time to head to Washington and avoid possible conflict with the ex-husband. I needed to leave before he had a chance to drive over after he got off work.

Driving away from town, miles outside of town, my phone rang. It was my boss! The office was closed. He had come in and signed the checks, but he refused to drop them at the mailbox. Demanding I return to mail them, I begged him not to make me come back for fear my ex would show up and there would be trouble. He laughed at me and let me know that if I did not return, I would be fired. Reluctantly, my new boyfriend turned the van around and headed back.

MISHA FAYANT

"I have a new mantra, which I chant softly to myself:
"Oh My God Oh My God."
Suzanne Finnamore

Moving as quickly as I could I gathered the checks and prepared to leave. My boss insisted I stay. He had some things to go over with me. Again, I begged to be set free. Impending doom settled over me, a dark feeling I could not explain. Finally, I was set free, but as I walked to the front of the store I could see through the glass the form of my ex-husband standing at my van, passenger door leading to the kids was open. Oh no!

Stepping out the front door, I apologized to him and said, "We need to go, it's getting late, and we will be back on Sunday."

"You're not going anywhere!" he growled back at me. "It's my weekend, and I'm taking the kids."

Calmly, I tried to reason with him, like a trainer trying to direct a lion. I explained the plan we had made and reminded him that Minda was looking forward to her annual birthday with Pappa just as she had always had.

In an instant, he snapped. Hitting me, he knocked me to the gravel driveway the van was parked on. As I grasped at the van pulling myself up, I watched as he grabbed my son and began tugging at him. Seat belt still on, he was choking my boy with the seat belt as he wildly attempted to extract him from the car. My arm shot between him and my son, trying to push him away and release my boy from the strap pushing around his throat.

LIFTED UP

Out of the corner of my eye I watched as my little girl dropped to the floor, crying, covering herself with pillows and blankets to shield her from the trauma.

More blows, but I did not move this time I was prepared. My arms were grasped so tightly they began to hurt as he tried to pry me out of the door, my body shielding the children.

Claude, my new boyfriend was stunned for a moment (Why, oh why, does no one believe me about this man and his temper?), but broke free of the shock in time to run around the end of the van before I could be thrown to the ground again. Shouting at my ex-husband to let go or deal with him, my ex turned to see this man 6' tall and 260 pounds of infuriated muscle. He paused only a moment before letting me go.

Now my boss was outside, too, calling the police as he walked out the door shouting at my ex-husband. Furious, my ex got in his car and drove away before the police could arrive.

Waiting for the officer to arrive, I looked down at my arms, bruises in the form of fingers wrapped around both arms showed purple against my pale skin.

Statements were taken from all of us, my boss, boyfriend, and I, before we were released to make our trip. It had been the afternoon I tried so hard to avoid. Furious at myself for returning and at my boss for insisting and threatening, my nerves would not allow me to stop shaking until we were an hour out of town.

Midway to our destination in the middle of the Central Washington plains, we pulled over at a rest area. Claude was so good with the kids and had them laughing and playing, putting the trauma of the day behind them. Inside the restroom, Minda and I washed our hands. Standing in front of the mirrors, I reached up to adjust my long hair in the heat. A shrill little scream suddenly came pouring from her mouth. I turned to look, fear hitting my gut like heated stones. "What? What's wrong baby?"

Tears welling up in her eyes, she cried, "Your arms, Momma, I'm so sorry, Momma!" I had forgotten all about the bruises that wrapped around my arms and extended from elbow to armpit. By now, they admittedly looked pretty gruesome.

My heart sank. I wanted so much to shield my babies from all the bad, but I was doing a horrible job at it. I wrapped my arms around her, hugging her tight and reassuring her that Mommy was okay.

Pappa's house was a welcome relief for all of us, between he and Claude the bad was washed away, at least for a few days. Claude did ask Pappa for permission, and then presented me with a diamond ring as he asked me to marry him.

Claude returned multiple times as we battled through court proceedings for the divorce. He was there with me at one of the first dates, when the pictures the officer took of my arms were presented. My ex's attorney was good and refused to allow the pictures to be shown in court but insisted they instead be viewed in a private room. I will never forget the look of evil on my ex's face as he sneered at me walking by to that private room with the attorneys to present the evidence.

"Taking a thing apart is always faster than putting something together. This is true of everything except marriage."
Joe Hill

Court was brutal. One day, walking in to that small-town courtroom in Sandpoint the new metal detectors were all set up. The hallways outside the courtrooms were bustling with attorneys and officials I did not recognize. Leaning in to my attorney, I quietly said, "Wow! What is going on here today?" She responded letting me know that all the excitement was about my hearing. It was the largest, most contested case in the area, and all these people were here to observe our case. My head reeled. What? Why? It was just a divorce!

Days and days, I was put on the stand and ripped apart by my ex's attorney. Every detail of my personal life was on display. Every man I had dated, had drinks, with even looked at was brought into question. It seemed I needed to know the full name, date of birth, and hometown of every male who was a part of my life.

Details were brought up that no one should have the right to know. Scanning my memory, I struggled to come up with a source for all this damning information. Then it hit me; my best friend, Connie. She had been an ex-girlfriend of my ex-husband before he and I got together. Through all her counseling of me to leave him, she was feeding him information on every little thing I did, even the things she encouraged.

One particular day near the end of my testimony, I turned the corner to the hallway that held our appointed courtroom at the end of it. The hallway was full to the gills of our friends, co-workers, acquaintances—nearly all of them apologizing, explaining they had been summoned and had no idea why they were to testify.

Inside the courtroom, my questioning had finally come to a close. It was my attorney's turn to question me. After all the lurid details allowed about my life, and me court was stopped abruptly when details about my ex came to light.

I had petitioned the court to remove his parents, as I did not feel they needed to hear the details of what we were about to delve into. Details about our sex life and oddities that I could not reconcile. Details about the pornography he kept hidden in the house. Pornography that portrayed things the Judge felt too "dicey" to continue.

The day was not even half over when the attorneys were called to chambers and a deal presented urged by the judge. One part of that deal was that I had to make a choice: I could move to Virginia to marry my now fiancé, but I would relinquish custody of my kids. Or

I could stay and though custody would be joint, I would be primary custodian of the kids.

"Divorce lawyers stoke anger and fear in their clients, knowing that as long as the conflicts remain unresolved the revenue stream will keep flowing."
Craig Ferguson

There was not a lot of thought to that. As much as I wanted to escape and as much as I thought I loved Claude, I could never give up my kids. How could I send them back to the den I fought so hard to pull them out of?

In the end, the agreement we came to materially was not much different from the one I had drafted a year before. Tens of thousands of dollars were racked up by attorneys on both sides. Money, as I pointed out to my ex, that could have gone to the kids, but now was wasted. All that money and a year of fighting for what? To come to the same agreement that I had drafted when this all began?

Anger and frustration were emotions I knew all too well. I had been ripped apart and laid bare; every sorted detail of my post marriage life was presented for all to see. He, however, was spared all that. Little did his parents, family, and friends know that the details he was spared baring would make mine seem weak in comparison. After all the years of degradation and abuse, I felt raped by that judge and the system. Dirty, unclean, and shamed were feelings mounting even through a proceeding that should have been liberating. Once again, I felt abused and violated.

LIFTED UP

Free! At least I was free of that marriage—free from the hell and control that had been the last 15 years of my life. It was time to write a new story.

"Divorce isn't such a tragedy. A tragedy's staying in an unhappy marriage, teaching your children the wrong things about love. Nobody ever died of divorce."
Jennifer Weiner

CHAPTER 19

CONSTRUCTING A NEW LIFE

"Only in the shattering can the rebuilding occur."
Barbara Marciniak

Divorce behind me, it was time to move forward to rebuild my life.

I spent the summer in California visiting my stepmom's family. The year I left my ex-husband, I discovered that his degradations of me were untrue. Men, even handsome men, paid attention to me. The one that began my road to a slice of self-esteem was a tall, dark, exotic man of Aztec descent. His notice, attention, and attempts to get my attention were all the flattery I needed to begin to realize that my ex-husband was wrong. I did not need to hide. I was not hideous and unattractive. He had told me no one else would want me and spent many days convincing me how damaged I was.

That Aztecan man was the memory I held to when old doubts crept in and the sound of my ex's voice filled my head.

The first few years post-divorce were volatile to say the least. The anger and animosity did not stop with the Judgement. They increased. Veiled and not so veiled threats continued to be made. Custody exchanges required a police escort. Many of them included desperate attempts by my ex to discredit me to the officers. The Officers who were so used to dealing with this kind of mess saw right through the dysfunction and corrected him time and again which only further infuriated him.

Part of the divorce proceedings included psychological assessments of both of the kids and us. Bullet points for me were: 1) I was a Martyr and needed to pull out of the self-destructive pattern. 2) My IQ was high 139, just below Genius level, and solidly in the "very superior intelligence" range, whereas his fell in the "normal" range.

Hearing that I was a Martyr brought out the Martyr in me, but it brought it to my attention and to the surface. It began a quest to overcome this unhealthy and unattractive trait. We had gone through a court ordered program called "Family Life Skills", a 10-week course targeted for men and women and taught differently for each. The focus for women was to overcome the martyr syndrome, (good news I was not alone, broken, and defunct like I had been told). The focus for men was to break the cycle of control and abuse. That class, along with the assessment, spring boarded me into healing.

The importance of the IQ portion was validation that my thinking was not broken! A case had been attempted to be built based on that injury to the head from high school where I was hit with a shot put. My ex told everyone I was "brain damaged" as a result. The story was that my thinking/reasoning could not be trusted, that I was incapable of even simple life decisions. This testing disproved all of that and documented that I was the more intelligent of the two of us.

For me, it was the beginning of believing in myself again. Reading the reports, it took years for it to really sink in. The report told a story that was opposite of the lifelong message I had been handed. That report, coupled with one generated by the department of employment which assessed me at the top percentage of every sector of the test and with some of the best scores they had seen in pattern reasoning, gave me space to believe in me.

That assessment gave me the courage to step into new roles and expand and use my knowledge even more.

MISHA FAYANT

Real Estate is the prime investment anyone can make. Working for that small construction company afforded me opportunities I might not have otherwise had. I learned all I could from the crews, supers, subcontractors, and suppliers. My boss finally began moving me into expanded roles at the business, allowing me to do some materials estimations, cabinet layouts and sales, and taught me to draw house plans.

Armed with all the knowledge I had been gleaning, I set out a plan to invest through real estate and secure a future for my kids and me. I was told thinking outside the box and seeing possibilities where others see obstacles was a strength I possessed. Searching for a lot to build on, I found that most were far out of my budget. Still I persisted. I spent evenings with the kids driving in search of a piece of land to build our home on.

We discovered a pie shaped slice of a lot with a challenging change in grade right in town. Due to its challenges, I was able to negotiate a price I could afford. Planning began. I spent every night after work devising a plan that would afford the kids and I everything we wanted, while fitting on the oddly shaped lot and allow for its steep and uneven grade.

I planned a 2,500 square foot home. My original drawings were sent to an artist to finalize them for presentation to the city for permitting and approval. The approval come all too easily.

School nights ended in our little family meeting at the lot working on the house at all phases until it became too dark to work. The kids and I were tired, but we built a beautiful home!

At work, increasing duties meant increased hours. The increase in hours was hard for my employer to swallow, so he made me the same deal he made with the construction crews. Any hours in excess of 40 hours were to be logged. Purchases could be made under the company for materials, supplies, and tools at the local hardware shop to account for the surplus in wages not paid on payroll.

Many of the materials for our house were garnered through this "deal".

LIFTED UP

As I grew my backbone back, it became an issue for my boss, who was used to the woman who said, "Yes, Sir" and let him push her too far. He had a reputation for being abusive to women employees. I had been called a loser in front of clients, fat shamed, harassed, and degraded in front of crews and clients alike. My employment there was soon to end.

"Start today creating a vision for yourself, your life, and your career. Bounce back from adversity and create what you want, rebuild, and rebrand. Tell yourself it's possible along the way, have patience, and maintain peace with yourself during the process."
Germany Kent."

Realizing opportunities for me in the small town were few, and wages were too little for most women in town to allow me to support my kids. I took my job search to Spokane. I would have to make the hour-long commute if I hoped to make enough money to support us all.

My small-town employer had lodged complaints with law enforcement making serious accusations towards me. I was cleared after spending time with the officers reviewing the documentation I had been smart enough to hang onto regarding my work and transactions.

He was a tenacious man, and I had angered him. Battles and more accusations flew. In the meantime, I was forced to pay back monies for the purchase of goods through that "side" log. Mediators were brought in, eventually with documentation, recordings, and other proof. I prevailed and was granted a good portion of the money's back.

In the midst of that turmoil, he came into question because of these dealings. An auditor was scheduled to review his records. As luck would have it, the records burned up in a "freak" fire that broke out in the attic of his business.

I began to wonder why I kept attracting this drama, these issues, and troubles. Were the scars in my heart and mind from childhood still causing me to have impaired judgement and decreased self-worth to allow these situations? How could I fix all that? The answers began trickling in, even if I did not recognize them for several more years.

A construction company in Spokane hired me to work as a bookkeeper, but soon sent me out to the field as a builder. I do not shy from challenges and knew I could do this. In reality, I was in a bit over my head. My schedules were based on the demands of the employer and not the reality of work onsite.

They were building 30 houses in a subdivision outside of the Central Washington town. The owners of the company held at least 4 other companies in LLC's and moved money between the companies as they saw fit. This meant soon there were conflicts and monies that should have been available to pay subcontractors were missing. At the end of the day, I transitioned to a new job, and this company still owed me over $30,000.

The employer had been involved in the Met Life scandal of the time and had far more experience and resources than I did legally. The back earnings were never recouped, and as a result, the beautiful house the kids and I had built was forced into short sale.

Heartbroken over the loss of the home we put so much heart and soul into; we packed our things and moved to Spokane. Even the proposal of this move caused great conflict with my ex, and back to court we went. Presenting the situation to the court, it was granted for me to move to Spokane even though it was further from my ex.

Then another construction company came into my life. This time, I was employed as a property manager for properties held solely by the owner and jointly with another businessman in town.

LIFTED UP

I had something new to learn: leases and commercial construction. Much of the knowledge I had gained up to now was put to use in my new position.

New job, new position, same employer M.O. Seemingly normal at the start, his cracks began to show. I heard stories of eccentricities, bullying, and ill treatment of female staff. My personality and my lifestyle pushed every button in his being.

Tempers flared one day, and as a result I was pushed into a wall and held there in front of male staff that stood watching not knowing how to react.

Still I stayed. I did not even question it. I needed to support my kids. This was the excuse I told myself for this new round of abuse by a new man. Somewhere deep inside, I began to recognize that I was drawing these relationships through the wounds that had been created so long ago.

Minda graduated and wasted no time in distancing herself from me. Following my lead, she ran to Central Washington to a man who she hoped could save her.

Minda and I were at odds about nearly everything during those days. As much as I wanted to be a good mother, I was not healthy. I had to realize that my own wounds and need for love and attention were dysfunctional.

Men came in and out of my life as I searched for that one who could see my worth and accept me. The problem was if I did not see my own worth, no man was going to magically find it for me. The kids did not fully understand the pain I bore deep within, the grasping need for someone in my life, or the pain I felt at being alone and unloved. Somewhere inside, I feared that Mom had been right—no one would ever love me. I just was not good enough. That searing fear drove me to frantically seek out someone who could love me.

A healthy relationship had not been the model for my life. Mom taught me to stress eat, to stress spend, and to seek out the attention of men when I was feeling insecure. Pappa taught me to be a smart ass, to get up when knocked down, and to never give up. As much as I love Pappa, I will admit there were times I felt abandoned even by him. Those days were filled with a crippling fear.

CHAPTER 20

LETTING PAPPA GO

*"My father gave me the greatest gift
anyone could give another person,
he believed in me."*
Jim Valvano

Tracy Chapman and John Mellencamp, Marty Robbins and Charlie Pride. Their music makes me think of Pappa. I remember being shocked that he knew who Tracy was and that we both listened to her deep soulful music. He and I had such a deep connection. He was my hero in every sense of the word. My love for him is beyond words, and even as I write about him, there are tears flowing—a deep sense of pride and a smile and a giggle all rolled into one ball of emotion.

The car was packed with three little souls and myself. Okay, they were teenagers and not so little: my daughter, Minda; my son, Damon; and their close friend, Julia. The car was full of suitcases, coolers of food, music, and anticipation.

Just a day before I had received a call that would rock my world and drop me to my knees. Pappa was in intensive care in Minnesota and not expected to make it much longer. Panic had struck. I did not think I could go. My manager at work, Vickie, was such a kind, giving soul. She came to my office and quietly looked at me with so much compassion and said "Go. You have to go. Just take the time and go."

I held it together long enough to wrap up what I was working on and make my exit. Once in the car, torrents of tears came pouring out between soul shaking sobs.

I called the kids and told them we were making the drive to Minnesota. Minda's friend came because she wanted to support Minda through the grief.

Pappa was the center of all our worlds. He was the cement that filled our cracks and made us stronger. We were all in disbelief. He was supposed to be invincible! This man, our hero, had survived being pronounced dead something like seven times throughout his life. Every time he got knocked down, he got up stronger. How could he be leaving us?

Through the blur of pain and fear, we focused enough to gather together and hit the road. The trip across Montana was never ending—the road long and mountains. The girls and I took turns driving because we had no time to stop. Somewhere past 24 hours, we finally made it to Minnesota and made our way to the hospital where Pappa was being cared for.

Tension built, along with excitement pulling into the parking lot. I missed him so much and could not wait to see him, but then the reality of why we were there came crashing through.

So many memories, so much joy juxtaposed to the pain, my head felt full. My mind has this weird coping mechanism, taking me through multiple movie screens of life all at once, to distract me from the present crisis. Walking through the hospital searching for the unit he was assigned to, memories came crashing through like a thousand movie screens vying for position in my mind.

LIFTED UP

Memories of bright clear days and his smile that shone brighter than the summer sun. He had done his best to protect me during my days growing up. He knew the things I faced at home, the anger and spite and abandonment. He would often take me in his truck for adventures and respite from my home life. He was a long-haul trucker at the time, and he had this big beautiful cab-over truck, painted in a bronze and gold with a war bonnet insignia over the door. The inside was adorned in diamond tuck brown vinyl.

I proudly sat in the passenger seat, singing, laughing, and telling stories with him on those long trips. I learned so much from him during those days. I had no idea at the time that it was his effort to protect me and save me from a little more of the issues at home. It was not until much later that I realized what he had done for me.

He was just opening up fully to letting his heritage out. After years of being punished for being an Indian, he was standing proud in who he was and where he came from. He began teaching me more fully the spiritual ways he grew up with. He also began telling me stories of relatives and using the mixed language he grew up with, part Ojibwa and part French. It was an exciting time for me, full of love and knowledge.

Back to reality, we finally arrived at the floor and unit where Pappa was. Excitement and fear once again flooded over me. The doors to the ICU buzzed open and with a deep breath pulling in all the resolve I could muster, I stepped through.

The nurse's station stood in the center of the rooms that created the perimeter of the unit. I had not been given a room number, so I started to look through the glass of each room searching for Pappa. One room held a frail old man with little hair left on his head, gaunt and wrinkled. It was clear there was not much left of him. My heart rang out for that man, and I started to walk past until something caught my eye—my stepmom, Sinda, curled up in the back corner of the room.

NO! That could not be Pappa. He always had a head full of thick dark hair. How could this withering old man be my Pappa? I had just seen him the summer before and he looked fine, healthy, and wry as usual.

OH, this man. He had gone through knee replacement surgery a year ago. He called me after the surgery to rant about the "God damn idiots" at the hospital. They had put him on a gurney but did not strap him down or put rails up, then left him in the middle of a pre-surgical room. A technician came through and clumsily had bumped into the gurney jolting it abruptly. Pappa fell from the gurney and hit the cold floor, breaking his shoulder. His retelling was filled with rage and laughter. He somehow always found light even in the darkest corners.

"The problem is you think you have time."
Buddha

Later that year, he was working on his homestead in North Dakota, the piece of land his parents occupied when he was a small boy and was bitten by a spider. Of course, the bite was right on the knee that had just been replaced. That bite turned into an infection. That infection settled into the prosthesis that had just been implanted in his left knee. The infection led to him needing to have that prosthesis replaced.

To replace the knee a second time, they had to remove the prosthesis and replace it with a medication filled block to heal the venom spreading through the leg. Only when that infection was cleared could they install the new knee. He had been waiting for that infection to clear up, and in the meantime, ended up with pneumonia.

LIFTED UP

December was when the pneumonia settled in. He called me frustrated wanting that "damn block" out of his knee and to move on with life. His last Christmas was spent in the hospital bedridden. That man never sat still. I could hear the frustration in his voice. It was evident that he wanted up and to get moving. He had "shit to do!" It never even dawned on me to prepare to lose him at that point. He had always overcome obstacles, especially physical ones.

We talked, laughed, bitched, and told stories, both of us just "knowing" this was just a typical bump in the road. Somewhere in my gut, there was a warning, one I refused to listen to. A warning I could not bear to recognize.

The pneumonia never cleared, and he got worse over the next few months. That was when I got the call.

Now here I stood looking at this ghost of a man who molded my life. The man who taught me to stand up when I got knocked down. The man who told me to never give up. The man who took my hand and helped me find the silver lining in every cloud. How could it be that the vibrant man I loved so much was so quickly reduced to this man that I did not even recognize.

Looking at him, my gut felt as if it had been punched. I was horrified by the condition he was in. My mind reeled. There was cradle cap all over his head in the few strands of hair that was left there. Moving closer, I could see a tuft of hair that still carried that dark color I had so long been used to seeing. The rest of it was silver-white and so thin it could barely be seen through the cradle cap that covered his skull.

"You never know how strong you are,
until being strong is your only choice."
Bob Marley

Holding back tears, I walked in and took his limp hand, stroking it gently and quietly saying, "Pappa, I'm here. I love you so much." My eyes scanned the length of him, trying to take in the state that he was in.

This man was always so strong. Even in his 70's, he outworked men in their 20's. How could this have happened in just a few short months?

I was not prepared for that day. Standing there holding his hand, I just knew that I had to be strong. I had to help him like he had always had me. My internal talk was on overdrive, but the resounding thought was, "Stay strong. Stay strong for your Pappa."

Not long after I took his hand in mine, his eyes opened. There beneath those thin eyelids were the blue eyes I had always gained strength from. (My eyes turn blue every now and then, and it's then that I know he stands with me guiding me even today.) Those eyes still had some sparkle shining through the clouds of pain. He smiled and said, "There you are, my girl!" Instantly, I leaned in and hugged him.

As soon as I let go, he asked me if I would help him. I was always his helper, always the one he went to when he needed something he thought no one else could do.

The summer before, as if he had a premonition, he had given me directions as to what to do, where the insurance was, who to contact if anything happened to him. He told me "Your stepmom is not built for this. She cannot handle it. I need to know that you will take care of these things for me." I promised him that day not knowing how soon I would be held to the test.

Of course, the first thing he asked me to do was to brush his hair! He

LIFTED UP

gave a quick menacing glance across the room to Sinda who was still huddled in her near fetal position in the corner. "Finally, someone to take care of me!" he smiled at me and those eyes began to sparkle with that "coyote" energy he carried. I don't even know how long I stood there brushing his hair, cleaning that thick helmet of dry dead skin from his scalp. He always loved having his hair brushed, and even as a little girl I would stand behind him to brush it for him. You could see him relax, releasing the tension in him from head to toe.

The requests kept coming: he needed washed, he needed repositioned, and he just needed to be cared for. I was more than happy to help him with his every need. This man who taught me to be strong, who taught me to be gentle, who taught me to find joy, and be a warrior.

Within a few days he was doing much better and was moved to a new unit. By then, relatives had begun to show up. When Auntie Berniece and her girls came, his soul lit up. Those two had a brother/sister bond that was deep and lasting and transcended their differences.

Pappa had turned away from Catholicism because of the abuses he suffered as a child. Auntie, on the other hand, stayed steadfast in her religion. The only real thing they disagreed about was religion.

It felt like a rollercoaster ride those days. One minute, we had hope he would be back to the man we all knew and loved physically, the next moment a crew of doctors would come in stripping that hope away.

One day, so many doctors came into the room to discuss his condition that there was not enough room for all of us to be in there. I had stepped aside to allow his wife to take the helm. I thought she would step up and listen to what the doctors had to say, ask questions, and get involved. Instead, she sat not moving in her same fetal position in the new corner.

I had enough. I could no longer try to be diplomatic with this woman. I was his daughter, and I was going to do something. I turned to her and asked, "Are you going to go find out what's going on? If you're not, I'm going to."

She just looked at me with a zombie-like look and said, "Okay". I know she was overwhelmed, but I could not fathom how she could just detach so completely from his care.

Determined, I stepped into the circle of doctors and asked them to recap what was going on. I was not prepared for the answers.

The reason he had not been healing from the pneumonia was because he had lung cancer!

I was devastated and enraged all in one, both building like a burning fire in the pit of my gut. Lung cancer was a damning diagnosis, but I was furious, because for 30 years I had tried to get him to stop smoking.

Even with this declaration of diagnosis, the only thing Sinda seemed to be able to think about was that she needed a cup of coffee and a "ciggie". Seriously? The news was just delivered that he has lung cancer and your first thought is, "I need a cigarette?"

Re-centering, I began to ask questions. I learned that there was hope for recovery for him. He seemed to be doing so well. They would devise a plan to deal with the cancer but could do nothing about his knee until that was dealt with.

LIFTED UP

*"We must accept finite disappointment,
but never lose infinite hope."*
Martin Luther King, Jr.

Both Pappa and I did not seem to fully integrate the gravity of the news. We just focused on the "hope" piece they gave us and trudged forward.

The kids and I were there for nearly 2 weeks. During that time, he would not let anyone touch him. The kids and I turned him every few hours, repositioned, cleaned, and administered meds with the watchful eyes of the nurses on staff. He bragged about how no one could care for him better than his girl and her kids.

We took great pride in those words! We took turns doing whatever was needed. Damon sat by his head and cleaned him up after every coughing spitting episode, and he did it like a champ, never once shying from the duty. Minda sat near and gave him her best butterfly energy (she is butterfly clan). We all did our part to heal him.

He was not initially able to eat or drink anything, and slowly we were given the okay to give him sips of coffee. No one else dared give him what he asked for, so I would stand and deliver for him. I always gave caution for him to not overdo it.

One nurse told me that he could have hard candies, as long as we watched him, and he did not begin coughing too much. Apparently Sinda did not hear any of the conversation. He asked for a candy and a sip of coffee, to which I obliged. Sinda nearly lost her mind, screaming at me and trembling.

Not long after, we took the kids and ran to the store for food and supplies. Once the kids all crawled out of the car, she stayed behind with me in the car. She began yelling at me that I was killing my father and that she would never forgive me.

I yelled back! "IF he is going to die, then I'm going to give him some comfort. I'm not going to have him suffer if that is what is going to happen! The nurse told me it's okay. It's not my fault you can't cope and have no idea what is going on."

With a red face she climbed out of the car slamming the door behind her yelling, "I will never forgive you! If he dies, it's all your fault!"

I was so angry at her for her incompetence and selfishness. Part of me laughed at her feeble attempts to regain control. She always hated the closeness between Pappa and I. I think she was threatened by our bond, and often was irrationally jealous of it.

A friend of the family had told me years before, she told them she was getting a kitty. You see, I am allergic to cats and she was aware of that. She apparently told them that if she had a cat, I would not be able to come visit.

My funds were stretched, and it was time to return home. At the end of those two weeks, the prognosis looked brighter. I did not want to leave, but I was almost out of money and had to get back to work. With a heavy, sad heart, I delivered the news to Pappa that we would have to be heading home soon.

I could see in his eyes that he did not want us to go, a kind of masked pleading. Something he tried to glaze over to not make me feel bad. He smiled and said he would be fine, that we should head home.

I remember our last hug. I did not want to let go and neither did he, but he pushed me away and said, "Go, get these kids home. I'll be fine."

Back in the car we all went, three kids and I, to make the long trek home. The kids did more driving than me on the way back. I was emotionally drained. There was a gnawing, eating away at my intuition that I should not have left. Reality conflicted with that saying I had to provide for my kids. My head felt like a pinball machine bouncing back and forth between guilt of leaving and the "what if's" and the hard reality of what I must do to provide.

Reports kept coming in that Pappa was doing well. He was being scheduled for procedures to deal with the cancer. It gave some relief and I held on to hope, but that gnawing never fully went away.

One week after returning home I received a phone call from the hospital. Pappa had taken a turn for the worse and was back in ICU. There was no longer hope. It was inevitable.

The voice on the other end of the line was telling me that my stepmom was incapable of giving them direction, and as next of kin, they wondered if I would take on the responsibility. All the resolve in the world filled me in one instant. Pappa and I had this talk many times, and I was well aware of what he wanted.

I was told we could prolong his life continuing life support protocols, or we could give him comfort and remove them and let him go. Without hesitation, I told them to stop all support except for comfort measures. It was a decision I stood in confidence of. I knew with all my being that it was what he wanted.

Hanging up the phone, I quietly walked to my room shut the door and cried for hours.

That night, my son came down to comfort me and sit with me. The soft glow of the television was the only light in the room as we sat in silence. Somewhere in the late hours, we fell asleep to that glow.

Early in the morning I woke, startled. As my eyes began to focus, I could see the shape of Pappa standing by the bed. His voice softly filled the morning air. "Baby girl, I'm tired, I want to go now, but I need to know you will be okay." His voice was so gentle and sweet; full of the caring he had always held me in.

"Go rest now."

Still a bit drowsy and not fully aware, I smiled, and responded out loud, "Of course, Pappa, I will be fine. You go rest now."

Damon woke to the sound of my voice questioning whom I was talking to. By then the image of Pappa was gone. I reached out to hold my son and said, "It's okay."

Within a half an hour, my phone began ringing. It was Sinda, sobbing hysterically. I could barely make out what she was saying. Pappa was gone! I sat up straight, and asked, "What? When?" The response was that he had passed just about half an hour ago. The time was right after I had seen him standing in my room.

I remembered he had told me the story of when Grandpa went "home". Pappa said that he was standing in front of a mirror in a truck stop. When he looked in the mirror, it was not his face he saw, but the face of Grandpa, who said, "Buddy, I'm going home now. I'm going to be with Ernestine."

I was comforted that in the moment of transition, Pappa came to make sure I was okay before leaving this life. It's a memory most won't understand or comprehend, but one that solidified our bond and love.

LIFTED UP

There was great comfort in that grief, knowing that I had gotten to say goodbye. Knowing that he was able to go rest because I was not selfish in holding him here. I held to that conviction for years.

I knew I had done the right thing without question. Or did I? The rational side of me knew it was what he wanted. Still I have carried a deep guilt and remorse for that decision. I still know it was the right thing, but it does not stop the pain of the burden of that decision to take his life.

"My DAD.
My father is a man like no other.
He gave me life, nurtured me, taught me, dressed me, fought for
me, held me, shouted at me, kissed me, but most importantly he
loved me unconditionally.

There are not enough words I can say to describe just how important
my father was to me, and what a powerful influence he continues to
be.

I LOVE YOU, DAD."
Unknown

CHAPTER 21

THE FUNERAL

*"When he died, all things soft and beautiful and bright
would be buried with him."*
Madeline Miller

Home less than two weeks, and I needed to head back to North Dakota. Now what!? I was tapped financially and had no idea how I would make it to his funeral.

Plane tickets were out of the question. Belcourt is nowhere near an airport. Driving was also out of the question. I could not do the 20-hour drive alone safely. I was too exhausted already. I checked the bus, but it would take too long. The train seemed to be the only option to get me anywhere near Belcourt on time. Even so, how? I had no money left to buy the ticket.

Slumped in my chair, I sat wondering what I would do. I saw movement out of the corner of my eye and looked up. There stood the small in stature but gigantic in heart manager I worked for. Vickie knew my situation. She could not bear to see me miss my Pappa's funeral. Trembling, but with command, she reached out and handed me a check.

"Just don't say anything. Take it and go." I tried to refuse, but she insisted. I called the kids and talked with each one separately. They both declined the trip back to North Dakota. I think they could not bear the goodbye.

MISHA FAYANT

Sitting in the dark on the near empty train, memories came flooding through. I tried to find a seat away from other passengers, a place where I could breakdown if needed. I could not help but think the other passengers thought I was crazy. I would go from smiling, giggling to tears streaming and refusing to make eye contact.

*"Death leaves a heartache no one can heal,
love leaves a memory no one can steal."*
From an Irish headstone

Headphones and music tracks, including Pappa's favorites, flooded my ears for hours, drowning out the reality of the world around me.

Grief is an irrational thing. Somewhere along the ride, a handsome young man climbed on the train. He was brave enough to strike up conversation with the lone woman in the back of the car we occupied.

He made me smile and made me laugh. For a few hours the pain subsided.

Oddly, there was something I took pride in from our "genetics". Pappa had charisma that was undeniable, and even in his late years; women half his age sought him out. He always stood proud in the sexual power of the Fayant bloodline.

It only seemed natural to relish in the relief of the chance encounter on the train. It was a release of tension and sadness and an escape to a more exciting place for a few hours.

In the early morning light of the North Dakota plains, I departed the train. A cousin called my name and rescued me from that strange silence and foreign place.

We had met the summer before when I had gone to see Pappa. Terry was rebellious and free spirited, so much like Pappa.

I must have been beaming from the diversion. She asked what had happened, and I gladly retold the story of the encounter with the dark, young man from the train. She just laughed, slapped my leg and said, "Your dad would be proud!"

The rest of the trip to the reservation was spent in story and catching up with each other. It made the drive seem instant.

Family, which on the reservation means EVERYBODY, came and went, bringing food, prayers, and condolences. It seemed everyone knew and loved Pappa. He was vibrant, cocky, smart, mischievous, and loving all in one. He did not take "crap" off anyone, but he was always there to help when needed.

Our days were spent visiting relatives and hearing stories about him and his antics. Our evenings were spent visiting with cousins and drinking, trying to numb the pain and be strong.

Things were tense at the house. My stepmom was broken and lost, wanting to be strong, but losing all control. I think she hated my presence more than ever. She tried so hard to stand up and take the reins but could not hold on to them. She would give me tasks and then be angry with me for doing so much. Grief, it's so unpredictable.

Packing Pappa's things, deciding what to keep and what to let go of, ended up being the biggest source of conflict. I took things that the kids and I had bought for Pappa and things that the kids and I would hold dear and have remembrance of him for.

It felt like a hundred bees swarming me during that time. Upset that she had wanted to give some things to HER grandkids, she lashed out at me in anger and pain. Frustration and anger welled up inside me. I was his daughter! I had been in his life longer than she had. The things I was taking were things I bought for him.

Tired of the stinging from her venom, I turned and lashed back at her. Simply, succinctly I said, "You are more than welcome to give your grandkids the things THEY gifted him! Oh! There aren't things they gifted him with? That is not my problem. These things the kids and I got for him will return home with me!"

She stood stunned and breathless for a moment. Suddenly that silence turned into more chaos. Items that I had made or given him came flying at me as she went through the room hurling his belongings my way.

I did not want to fight. It was not my intent to hurt. This was MY Pappa, and I was tired of being pushed out of his life and now even the act of grieving for him by this woman. I just wanted to grieve, to hold onto a few things that were special to the kids and me. Things we bought or made him with love. How could she even think to deny us those things?

The sad truth was, Pappa had come to me and told me he wanted to leave her but felt obligated to stay because she had been there for him some 20 years earlier. So many conversations with him hung in the back of my mind as this little woman bit at my ankles angry with me for the love that bound Pappa and I together. A love she never had with him and knew it. What she did not understand was, in his own way, he loved her all he could and in ways that kept him from his own happiness.

He was not perfect. He had affairs. She never knew. She never lifted her head enough past her own feet to see. A tornado was building in my soul, a dark whirling mass ready to eat up all in its path. My limit had been reached. One of us had to give; I took my leave and went driving with my cousin. Visiting places that were dear to Pappa. Visiting more relatives. Searching out drummers for his wake. At least

LIFTED UP

when I was with Terry, I could celebrate his life. Laughter returned.

I began to dread going back to the house. I felt like a great Mastiff with a chihuahua biting at my ankles constantly. My head felt like a great jug filled with water, sloshing, heavy, distorting sounds that came in. Numbness crept through my bones so quietly I did not recognize it at the time.

My chest was laden with the weight of a ton of the thick clay that covered our ancestral grounds. I felt I could not breathe. All the tears and emotion within me being held down to honor the strength Pappa would have wanted out of me. The downside was, I did such a good job that others forgot that I was grieving, too.

The ground beneath me seemed to be breaking, opening to swallow me whole. Everything was unstable. Confronted by a relative I did not yet know, I stood body numb, heart raging like a wildfire.

The words coming at me seemed so impossible and ridiculous, I had a hard time grasping what was being said. I was being told that Sinda had gone to friends and told them I was stealing from her! With clarity, I spoke in as calm of a tone as I could muster and assured them that the only things I possessed where those things which I had given Pappa. The insults towards me continued to which I coldly and directly invited them to come to the house with me directly and check my possessions for these "stolen" goods.

To no surprise, they declined. Keeping a calm but stern voice, I explained that I was his daughter, that his wife was grieving and incapable of coping. I gave them an invitation to take pause and think things through before tossing out blind accusations.

Darkness had settled over the reservation. The light in the sky from the moon and stars was all that lit our path home. Inebriated from the night with my cousin, we headed to that little house tucked in the Belcourt woods. Rage and burning anger were not masked by the copious drinks I had taken in over the course of the night. Hurt and fury stirred in my soul bringing forth a monster that even I would be afraid of. My resolve to be kind and even keeled was being put to its ultimate test.

She had waited up for me. As soon as the door opened, the chihuahua began nipping, and the mastiff finally barked back! I had enough! Veins popping from my neck, hands clenched, I commanded her to back off. This was a side of me she had never had directed at her before. The chihuahua quieted to a whimper, tucking tail and running to her room.

From the safety of her room, she began shouting again. Clearly, she was as drunk as I was. At the opposite end of the house, I stormed into my room and slammed the door behind me with a resounding boom that shook the house. I wanted to cry, hurt and wounded by her words and false accusations, but infuriation and alcohol held my tears prisoner. Only a few more days, and I was gone anyway.

"It hurts when they're gone. And it doesn't matter if it's slow or fast, whether it's a long-drawn-out disease or an unexpected accident. When they're gone the world turns upside down and you're left holding on, trying not to fall off."
Walter Mosley

Pappa had expressed his wants to me before he passed. He wanted to make sure my kids had certain items of his. Among them were a rifle and fishing pole for my son, and a belt buckle for my daughter. His words were stern when he made me promise to make sure they got these items.

After the accusations, I was threatened with the police if I touched anything that belonged to him. I began devising a plan. Nothing was going to prevent me from doing what I promised my father, not even this woman who turned so vile in her grief. I waited quietly until she was gone one day and searched the property for the items he spoke of. One by one, I found them.

Body shaking, heart racing, I felt like a criminal! That feeling then opened the door for more fury. Why the hell should I feel like a criminal? She should not still be his wife except for his pity for her. We were his blood family, the ones who had always stood by him. How could she be making this so hard? Why should I feel so dirty and wrong for completing my father's wishes?

Knowing I could not keep the items anywhere she would suspect, I loaded his old pickup truck (which was left to my son) and drove up that bumpy, dirt road to a place where there were fallen trees and brush near the road. Everything was placed in plastic bags and tucked under the tree, covered by the brush. Mother Earth would have to hold his wishes tight until I could return for them in a day or two.

In tandem with all this mess came dealing with the church. Pappa's sister had promised him a priest for his funeral. How and when this change occurred, I had no idea. Now I had to balance the wishes he told me with the demands of the church. More stealth? How could one funeral cause so much intrigue?

Pappa had told me from the time I was young and up to his end, that he wanted to be cremated and his ashes spread over the land he grew up on. The church demanded a burial and a grave site, or they would not perform services or allow his funeral at the chapel Auntie B was intent on.

Lord! My every skill was being tested. I met with the priest and Auntie. There were so many questions about his burial and when it would be and threats of cancelling the service if I did not comply. I had to come up with a story on the fly to convince them their wishes would be fulfilled, all the while knowing that Pappa's wishes did not match.

It was nerve wracking and soul wrenching, lying to a priest and my Auntie. I did what I felt necessary to make all things happen on this little reservation.

Pappa was prepped for viewing. Knowing that he had asked for my daughter to receive his turquoise eagle belt buckle, Sinda placed it on his corpse. SHIT! Could this get more complicated? Heart racing yet again, mind turning over multiple possibilities, here I was once again devising a plan. It felt like Pappa was standing over me smiling, testing his girl, and I could not let him down.

Once the public viewing was complete and Sinda was taken away by friends, I turned and went back to the funeral home. I asked to see his body one more time. Tremors began rattling my bones, sobs and tears poured from me as I leaned in and gave him one last kiss. Hand trembling, I reached out and gently touched his cold cheek. "I love you, Pappa," I said aloud between breaths and tears.

The mortician had told me to take the belt he graciously departed the room knowing what was happening. Hands quaking, I unbuckled the belt and slipped it from his lifeless body, rolled it and tucked it under my shirt. As I turned to leave, the mortician gave me a compassionate nod, laid his hand on my shoulder and softly said, "You did what he wanted. Go in peace." More tears! How could one set of eyes produce so many damn tears?

""I love you every day. And now I will miss you every day."
Mitch Albom

CHAPTER 22

VALIDATION

"If you live for people's acceptance,
you will die from their rejection."
Lecrae

Sitting at my computer wasting time on Facebook one afternoon, a friend request came through. It was an old friend from my childhood in Northern Idaho. I was so excited. It had been a long, long time since I spoke with anyone from that small town. The hurt, pain, memories of loss kept me from having any wish to return to my hometown. I drove through it from time to time on my way to Montana, but never really had any reason to go back.

I accepted the request. A conversation was struck up and, of course, memories and stories from "the old days" were shared. Finally, she asked me how I was. I was a bit confused, as we had been talking back and forth for a while now. Then she asked more pointedly, how things were with my mom and me.

A big hole of darkness had just been opened. Even in my 40's, I struggled with the relationship. I loved my mother so much yet, felt so much anguish over the things that had happened in my life. I felt my body tremble and heave uncontrollably. The faucets that are my eyes let loose with a torrent of tears as we talked.

There is a part of me that wants to make sense of everything, no matter what it is. I remember struggling so much with the stories of my life, because my brothers and my mother told me that every story I remembered was wrong. I was vehemently told that I lived in a fantasy world of my own making. I really began to feel as if I was as crazy as they said.

I unpacked the story of how I had spent time going back to my hometown to seek out neighbors to ask what they remembered of our family. I had spent so many years being told that I was not right in the head, that I did not remember correctly, and that I was crazy. I felt a need to find clarity for my sanity.

"Everybody is looking for validation,
no matter who you are,
and I think that's a need of the human condition –
to look for affection or recognition or validation.'
Alejandro Gonzalez Inarritu

I had gone back to my hometown, before I turned the age of 20, on a quest for truth. I sought out the people, neighbors, parental friends, and childhood friends that I remembered being a part of our life. I wanted to know the truth. I needed to know if I was really crazy and as broken as my family had constantly told me.

One by one, I found the key people who were involved in our lives. One by one, I sat down with them face-to-face when possible, by phone or email when not. My request was simple. I asked each and every one of them for the same thing. I asked them to tell me what they remembered of our family; it's dynamics, and what they remembered of my childhood and the person I was. I asked them for the truth as they remembered and not just what they thought I wanted to hear.

LIFTED UP

I would impart on them how much I needed truth and clarity to be able to move forward with peace in life. I wanted to make sure that I remembered clearly and not live in some made up fog of a life that was not real.

One-by-one the stories came in. Almost always, they matched to what I remembered as being truth. Once in a while, pieces were given to me that I had not recognized as a small child or differed slightly from what I recalled. But overall, the stories resonated with my memories. Little by little, I found the relief that I had been looking for. I was not crazy! The events of my life, the way they happened, and the dynamics of our family were being relayed back to me very closely to how I remembered them. Armed with this knowledge, I began to heal that piece of me.

It was very empowering to my young soul, and even today, to know that I had not made up a construct of martyrism as I had been told. It was freeing to know that my mind was not the damaged, defunct construct that I had been nearly convinced it was. A weight lifted, a looming cloud that covered my life and clarity, my will to live and grow, started loosening itself from my soul and rising from my shoulders, allowing me to take meaningful breaths for the first time in many years.

One day, my older brother was arguing with me. He was doing his best to let me know how damaged I was. He told me again and again that nothing was the way I remembered it. He told me I made stories up to suit my need to be a victim. When I told him that I had in fact contacted these many people from our lives and spent time talking with them, he was shocked. He looked at me vehemently, and at the same time his eyes sparkled.

I imagined that he thought I would relay how I was wrong, and they confirmed it. I then told him that their stories were in alignment with my memories, and that I was, in fact, not the one with memory issues. His appearance changed from the cocky, victorious stance he had been holding to one of disbelief and rage. The response from him was anger-filled. He told me that I had just been told what I needed to hear from these people. "Of course, they are not going to tell you the truth," he would say. "They are going to tell you what they think you want to hear. You fool! You got nothing from them. You're still damaged!"

As a younger woman, I had this intense need to be right. Maybe it was because I did feel so flawed and damaged I just needed validation. I began to realize, that no matter how much proof I provided, certain players in my life were never going to be able to accept my truth, my story. It would mean rearranging their belief system, maybe changing their views on who they idolized, or forgiving someone that they long held animosity toward, or admitting to actions by themselves that were not at all pleasant to face.

That friend that wrote was the first of a string of many who re-found me several years ago. Those months, that year of re-acquaintance with these childhood friends who poured into my life from nowhere was so healing and empowering for me. It was finally a year of "you're not crazy!"

One-by-one, friends were added via Facebook, which was an unexpected Godsend. Each time a friend was added, our talk went back to our childhood. Each time, it was inevitable that they would ask how I was doing and how my life had been since leaving that small North Idaho town. At first, I felt like it was just normal conversation. Then I began to realize a pattern was developing.

As our conversations continued, nearly every one of them relayed to me of how happy they were that I was "okay." A few of them shared with me something that was hugely shocking to me then and even now—they prayed for me. I was often the subject of their family's prayers. Families were worried that one-day they would find out that I was no longer among the living. To put it short, they worried that my life would have been ended far too early.

LIFTED UP

I was shocked! Remember for years I was told that none of these things happened to me? That my life was not what I remembered? That I was mentally defunct? Now as an adult and many years away from that life, people were seeking me out. People were relaying stories to me of what they remembered. These requests, memories, and stories were coming in unsolicited by me. With each one, I felt a little more empowered, a little less broken, and a whole lot less crazy.

"To see yourself, and for others to see you, is a form of validation. I'm interested in that very mysterious and mystical way we relate to each other in the world."
Mickalene Thomas

The first time I was told that I had been the focus of many, many family prayers; torrents of tears flooded my face momentarily blinding me. I felt like I was standing at ground zero of a major earthquake. My world. My story was shaking loose from the rock walls that held me down for so many years. It shook me to my core.

It is one thing to believe you remember something and to believe it with your entire heart and soul against all odds and objections. It is entirely another thing to have it validated after a lifetime of cover up and being told that you are mad as a hatter. The tears felt as if they were washing away some deep held stain from my soul. Tears cleansed my soul and rinsed away the smudges on my heart.

When I asked why I was the focus of prayer, the answer was that most every family back then knew that I suffered abuse and neglect. Those families truly feared that they would pick up a paper one day and find my obituary. So many emotions boiled up: anger, relief, joy, despair. You see, that was a different time and place. When I was a child, people did not report things, they prayed. There was no

240

agency to alert and no system for protection of a child that was prevalent.

Once the tears stopped, I broke down in hysteria. It felt like a pressure valve had been released. Years of self-doubt and layered mental abuse began to slough off. I felt like a butterfly being born from the caterpillar's cocoon, to find light, fresh air, and a new lease on life. I truly believe that these conversations were the beginning to the healing of my deep, debilitating depression.

The ego in me wanted so badly to take these conversations and shove them down my brother's throat. By now though, I realized that nothing I said, no amount of proof would ever change his mind. He was entrenched in his recollection of my life.

I had to let go of that need to be right, at least in the eyes of those family members who were incapable of seeing any truth but their own. I had to come to terms with the fact that I most likely would never get the acknowledgement from them that I had waited for my entire life. I had to realize that the only person who really needed that confirmation was me.

I realized that my immediate family would likely go to their graves holding to their beliefs. I was fortunate enough to have the help of some beautiful souls in my life. I began to come to terms with the fact that it was okay! I could let go of my need to be right in the eyes of my family. I could move forward in my own life.

That year was a huge turning point for me. I had lost my father. It felt like he had been the only other person to validate my memories. I wanted so much to share all these revelations with him, but he was gone. No sparkling blue eyes to smile back at me and give me words of encouragement. No rough, work-worn hands to reach out and take mine and tell me I was okay. That year was a gift from the Universe, in the absence of my father, just when I needed some sanity and comfort, in just the right moment to help me begin to heal.

LIFTED UP

Those contacts, those validations, were enough to let me begin to put the fractured pieces of my brain and heart back together.

It is curious to me that this all occurred right about the time I began powerlifting. All the clearing, all the validation, along with the physical strength that was being built began to give me back my own personal power. I had been hiding from it for so long, and it felt so amazing to be reclaiming my power once again.

It was amazing to be able to say "YES! I survived. YES! I am still alive! YES! I am not crazy!" and, of course, there was the not so small part of me that said, "YES! I WAS/AM right!"

"The only permission, the only validation and the only opinion that matters in our quest for greatness, is our own."
Dr. Steve Maraboli

MISHA FAYANT

CHAPTER 23

FINDING STRENGTH

"You gain strength, courage, and confidence by every experience in which you really stop to look fear in the face. You are able to say to yourself, 'I lived through this horror. I can take the next thing that comes along."
Eleanor Roosevelt

I had fallen into mirroring for my kids exactly the things I wanted them not to learn. Still that broken girl inside me could not let go of the dysfunction. Clamoring for acceptance, there were days and nights, months, and years that I am not proud of.

Home was now just my son and me. My dysfunction was even starting to drive him away. I fell back into the nights of crying in depression begging God to take me away. He wanted to go live with his Dad. As much as I loved my kids, I was slowly driving them away. Desperate at the thought of them both being gone soon and me being all alone, I struggled.

My past wounds came back with a vengeance, and the nightmares began again. I was crumbling piece by piece. The kids saw it, even if no one else did. They saw more than any child should have to as my heart and mind melted deeper into that depression, born of the fear that my prophecy had been told years before.

The mess inside me drove my little girl further from me. It broke my heart as I feared repeating the relationship I had with my own mom. I wanted better for her but did not have the skills to get there. All that pain drove her to a relationship with a man who I feel mirrors my ex. Charming to the world, he was controlling at home, and I fear far more abusive than I could imagine. Still, she needed escape from the chaos that was her Mom at the time. It was not long before she conceived my first grandchild.

I poked my head up out of the dysfunction long enough to glimpse the reality of kids who could no longer bear being near me. I made feeble attempts to reclaim some space in their hearts.

My son, Damon, loved football. It was his great passion. I made sure I went to all his games. With all my might, I tried to be the Mom he needed yet I failed him so horribly in other ways. I had made sure we lived in the boundaries of one of the best schools in Spokane. This meant that the football team was ranked somewhere around 10th in the entire nation. Making the team was no small feat, getting field time was even more difficult.

Damon had the vision of his Pappa and I. He could just see things, movement, and patterns that gave him an advantage on the field. To his disadvantage, he was neither big nor quick. Unfortunately, it was speculated that other boys had begun using steroids to be competitive. This speculation came as the boys bragged about it. It was not an option morally for Damon or me. We had to devise another plan and work with what we could.

Gold's Gym was positioned on the hill near his school. I got us memberships there and began taking him with me to try and build strength that would hopefully keep him relevant on this competitive team.

Upper body strength was his weakness. His legs were crazy strong. Writing a plan to build his upper body included lots of pressing movements, bench press, decline press, and incline press, among other things.

Bench press was the lift we were working on for the day. Sitting up, I could hear clapping from across the gym. I had put a 45 on each end of the bar, totaling a whopping 135lbs, laid on the bench and pressed it. Finally! I had wanted that number for a long time. The cheering and clapping came from a group of young men who had been watching, unknown to my son and me. It was an amazing feeling.

Lifting was my therapy. I felt strong, in control, and for that small amount of time, the broken woman was shoved aside.

"With the new day comes new strength and new thoughts."
Eleanor Roosevelt

We began going to the gym more frequently, both of us getting stronger. Coming out of the locker room to an impatient son, I saw him smile. A woman had come up to him and told him his mom was strong and that he should talk to her about taking up powerlifting.

Neither of us really knew what the sport was, we just knew it involved lifting and being strong. As soon as we arrived home, we both headed for the computer, determined to Google it and find out what "powerlifting" was.

Our search led us to discover that, even at my age, I could compete. Further research showed that I could break records. That was it! I was going to do it. We sat watching video after video, trying to learn what I needed to become a powerlifter.

Squats were already a part of our workouts. However, not like this! There were so many rules. The most glaring rule would be the "depth" rule. The hip crease had to drop below the knees, that was a long way down! It changed everything. Clumsily, we began working on it, not knowing what we were doing.

Bench press. I thought I had that lift under control. There were even more rules for this one, including the fact that the bar had to touch the chest and become motionless before a referee would give a call that allowed you to press it back up. That would take a lot of work!

Deadlift was the third and last lift. It looked simple enough—a bar on the ground with weights on it, you bend over and pick it up. Easy! I could do this.

Back in the gym, we began training; me for powerlifting and Damon continued his strength building for football. The woman who had started it all saw me trying to complete the lifts. Soon, she and her friends came to ask if I would like help. YES! Please!

Finally, I had a goal, something that did not involve family or taking care of others. It was a goal for me. I would become a powerlifter, and I would break records.

At that time, I was 45 and there was no such thing as "raw" powerlifting at a world level. Raw meant no supportive assistance gear other than a belt and wrist wraps. Equipped was the norm at the time, which involved tight fitting suits to help with the amount of weight you could lift and allowed knee wraps, used to give rebound out of the bottom of the squat and help the knees lock out at the top of the lift. I had no desire to lift in equipment. Damon and I decided we wanted to see what I could lift, not what the equipment could lift for me.

Walking into the gym, excitement and intimidation took turns coursing through me. It was my first powerlifting meet, a push-pull meet (bench press and deadlift only). Watching in awe as everyone warmed up, I felt so inadequate and new. Time to lift came sooner than I expected, and I was on the platform. I ended up walking away with a bench record and knowing that my deadlift needed to improve drastically.

Riding the high of my first meet the entire drive home, I knew I was hooked. It gave me focus, purpose, and a sense of self. I wanted so much more. I was told USA Powerlifting was THE organization to go with if I wanted to compete drug free and have the opportunity to compete on a world scale.

Winter came, and I competed in my first full meet, qualifying to compete at Nationals the next year. Training began in full earnest focused on competing at a higher level.

LIFTED UP

I had qualified for Nationals and had begun training in earnest to make the trip – the first step in my road to world competition.

Walking into the dark living room in search of the power cord for my laptop, I crept in trying not to disturb my sleeping son. Feeling around the table next to the couch, I located it and turned to walk quietly back out. That half-step turn changed everything. My left foot fell on a pillow tossing me off balance. Right foot reaching to find balance, it found another pillow instead. My ankle began to roll, and my weight shifted. I knew I was about to go down. Internal talk said just relax into it, so you don't get hurt. On the way down a boom rang out, followed by a loud crack. Feeling searing pain, I screamed and hit the floor unable to move my leg, my head numb from the pain shooting up my leg.

Damon jumped up from the couch terrified. He had thought he heard a gunshot followed by the sound of splitting wood. Scanning the apartment for the intruder, he stood in the dark confused as to what had happened.

He thought I had been accosted and shot. Reaching down to help me up once he realized all was clear, I could not get up. My leg throbbed. Moving it at all felt as if it was being ripped from my body. I needed a moment to clear my thoughts. Several minutes later, he helped me hobble to my room.

Lying in my bed, holding my breath every time I moved. I thought, "This must be the worst sprain I have ever had!" Three days later, Damon showed up at my door declaring, "Get up now and let me get you to the doctor or I'm leaving for Dad's for the weekend and you will have to wait until Monday." Neither of us knew how bad it was.

Gathering all the mental strength I had within in me, I slowly and carefully picked my leg up and made my way toward the stairs. It must have taken a half an hour to get down those stairs. Every movement made me want to die or wet my pants.

Hours later in the emergency room, we were told that I had torn the major ligament from my lower leg completely on one side (the sound of the shot gun) and the other insertion point was nearly torn off. That insertion point had caused so much stress on the fibula that it fractured it (the sound of wood splitting). A temporary cast was placed on that leg, painkillers given, and surgery scheduled for Monday to repair the ligament and bolt the lower leg together.

What timing! This meant no training for Nationals. I could not go that year, as I would be in a cast for 3 months. More importantly, my daughter was getting married in just a couple weeks. The reception was to be held in the garden area at the apartments. It was going to be a challenge helping her with all the preparations.

Thankfully, most of the tasks had already been completed. I would attend the wedding in a cast and be limited as to how much I could help that day. I had been instructed to keep the leg elevated. The fracture caused a deep vein thrombosis, and there was worry because of it.

Still working for that construction company, yet fully aware he was working to rid himself of me, my finances were tight. We planned the wedding to be held in the formal gardens at Manito Park. Doing all I was financially capable of, we planned a simple garden wedding and reception.

She wanted a simple wedding and reception. Mostly she just wanted family to get together. Her father had been tasked with bringing food from her favorite childhood market back in Newport. Mom offered to help by bringing in cake.

The day was beautiful, and my baby looked like a princess. The wedding was magical in those English gardens. Following pictures, we all headed to my abode for the reception.

Mom brought tons of food and needed my apartment for prep. Still on crutches and orders to stay off my leg, I had already been up too long. My leg was throbbing in pain. I went to the reception area to get off the leg and get it up, greeting the guests and supporting my daughter. Mom and family ran in and out of that third-floor apartment bringing out an endless array of food and cakes. It was way more than we had intended or planned for. Appreciating her efforts for my daughter, I allowed her reign of the reception. It had been a beautiful day.

LIFTED UP

Ah, but all too soon, I assumed that things were okay in our lives. Reports began coming in about how selfish I was, and how I had done nothing for my only daughter's wedding. I did not even help the day of the wedding! My older brother made Facebook posts about what a worthless, selfish woman I was making Mom pay for everything. I had done and paid for nothing. I could not read the posts, as I was not a friend on his timeline. Family and friends informed me of what was being said.

That all too familiar feeling hit my gut as if I had been punched followed by seething anger. He did not know my circumstance, and how dare she lie to everyone about the occurrences of that day. What should have been a beautiful memory for us all was turned into yet another family political battle. When and where would it end? What on earth had I ever done to have them hate me so deeply? Why would they ruin her day by acting this way?

I returned to work after the accident and the wedding to the crisis of 2010 and downsizing.

Training the people who would take over my job, I felt a mix of relief and shock. Even in this, I was so used to the cycle of abuse that I could not say no. We had just implemented a new software system, one that made total sense to me, but others struggled with it. The people remaining in the company were primarily family and a few key long-term employees. I chose not to take it too personal and did my best to rise above and leave on a good note.

Transitioning out of that company, I would be left at home alone. Damon had moved North to spend his senior year with his Dad in a school where he would be afforded much more time playing the game he loved so much. (His plan worked. He was a key player on the team and an anchor for it.)

Painting was a new hobby that I had taken up during that same tumultuous year, prompted by my healer friend, Carmen. Small in stature but mega sized in personality, she had taken me under her wing. She saw the creativity in me and pestered me to come paint with her until I relented.

I tested my skill out on a few small pieces before telling her yes. I began a series of large-scale angels in oil – go big or go home, right?

The first in the series was on a 3-foot by 4-foot canvas. A man crouched head down in prayer with massive wings furling out to either side of him. I had made the conscious decision to position all the angels so that a face was not seen. I did not want people to associate with a face, but with an emotion. It worked. Time and again showing my art at galleries and exhibitions, people would stop to share heartfelt stories spurned by the emotion the paintings elicited in them.

Those days were healing not only for them but also for me. I could pull myself out of the tears and depression enough to hear others and feel compassion for their pain. Feeling their pain gave relief from feeling my own. Hearing those stories kept my own demons at bay if even for a few moments.

Those transitional days from being a full-time Mom to being alone were filled with lifting and creating. It helped heal and deflect the pain building in my heart. I did not know how to be alone, but now I would face coming home to an empty house every day. Selfish needs did not want my son to go. Love for him pushed my needs aside to attempt giving him what he needed.

No one knows how much pain I felt watching him drive away with his car filled headed to go live with his Dad for that final school year. As soon as he was out of site, my door shut and locked, I fell into a heap sobbing uncontrollably. Abandonment issues that had nothing to do with him came bubbling up choking me suffocating on their way out. Would that pain ever end?

"Character cannot be developed in ease and quiet. Only through experience of trial and suffering can the soul be strengthened, ambition inspired, and success achieved."
Helen Keller

LIFTED UP

CHAPTER 24

ON THE MOVE AGAIN

*"No one saves us but ourselves. No one can, and no one may.
We ourselves must walk the path."*
Buddha

With a new grandson in the central Washington city of Pasco and nothing more holding me in Spokane, I moved to be closer to my little grandson who had stolen my heart. Dark hair, dark skin, coal black eyes, and never-ending energy, he made my heart smile.

Situated in my new home across the river from my new grandson and daughter, I began to settle into life in the Tri Cities.

It was discovered during my last visit with the orthopedic surgeon in Spokane that my hips were failing. My left hip had been bone-on-bone for a long time as far as he could see and would need to be replaced immediately. I was taking fistfuls of NSAIDs daily to try to cope with the pain.

A physician in the Tri Cities was enlisted and a total hip replacement was scheduled for September. A new, computer guided surgery was planned, minimally invasive with minimal scarring.

Floating in a hazy light, I drifted comfortably until as if being pulled by the back of my neck I came crashing down, slamming into my body. Pain! The most intense pain I had ever felt. What was going on? I could not speak, could not move, and the pain was mind numbing.

LIFTED UP

It felt as if I had been a victim in a horror movie, cut up with a chain saw, bound, and tossed in a casket buried underground where no one could hear my screams.

Eventually a low mumbled groan exited my lips, to which a nurse responded. I could hear her, but not see her. My eyes would not open. She said," I can't understand you, and I can't help you until you can speak clearly." Time and again she would come to the bedside repeating it, followed by a low laugh after tapping the side of the bed. "Bitch, this is no game!" I thought in my entombed state. Taunting continued until I could finally force my mouth and lips to form words.

She came back to my bedside, and with a sideways grin, asked what I wanted. I reached for her, shouting, "I want to punch somebody!" Stepping away, she just laughed and walked back to the nurse's station.

A new nurse came by to check on me and discovered that I needed something to mediate the pain. She asked questions about allergies before returning with something for the pain. As she administered it, she began to tell me that I had been given Narcan in the operating room. I had arrested. The Narcan flushes the entire narcotic out of your system. They were not sure what had made me arrest, but here I was. They were able to bring me back.

She was much kinder than the first nurse and attended to me with care.

Minda came to retrieve me from the hospital and deposit me at home. I had been given a huge triangular pillow that was strapped between my legs and was to be kept there. How would I get around? No matter, I was used to being alone. I spent days in my apartment post-surgery alone; finding what I could to eat and not letting the pain get too far-gone.

Standing in front of the mirror after the bandages were removed, I took a look at what had happened. That "minimally invasive surgery" left me with a 16" scar that resembled a shark bite nearly severing my left glute in half, another scar over 6" long was present on the front of my groin. What the hell? It was supposed to be a 3-inch scar front and back (approximately).

When I finally started walking I realized that my left foot turned in, so much that I kept tripping over my own foot as I walked. I called the surgeon's office and was told to just "force" the foot into a normal position it would eventually adjust. It never did. I tripped over that foot for 5 years.

"The world breaks everyone, and afterward, some are strong at the broken places."
. Ernest Hemingway

It took years and speculative deduction from other surgeons to come to this scenario.

When I arrested on the table, the surgeon had cut me open much further in order to quickly finish what he had started and put me back together as quick as possible. Thus, the grossly enlarged incisions and scarring, and the leg being put on crooked.

Work was scarce in the economic downturn. I had called the auto finance company and arranged for them to come get my car when I realized I would not be able to continue payments. Adjustments were made to make money stretch further. Every day was spent searching for employment to no avail. Waiting to speak to a counselor at the employment services office, I noticed a flyer for retraining to become a Medical Assistant. I immediately asked and was on my way to earning a degree that would put me back to work.

Just over a month post-surgery, I began college classes.

Enrolled in the yearlong intensive program, I was having fun. I love learning; love challenges, and pushed myself to earn the Dean's list, then the President's list at college.

LIFTED UP

That year was not quite what I expected from the standpoint of being a new grandmother. I remembered the unfettered access my parents had to their grandkids and expected the same to be true for me. Not so! My new son-in-law did not like me much and liked my presence in their lives even less. My time allowed with my grandson was greatly restricted and had to be scheduled. I could not "drop by" when in their neck of town.

It broke my heart. I felt hopeless, helpless, and frustrated. Living alone and restricted to once a week visits with my grandson, those old issues came stealing back in. Nights were spent in my bed crying so loudly I would feel bad for the neighbors and hung my head if I had to face them in the light of day.

I was so close to family but felt so very far away. The cycle of pain continued, and my heart broke a little more. I reminded my daughter of the privileges her grandparents had been afforded in her young life, to no avail. I did not realize at the time just how controlling and abusive her husband was. She did not dare tell me. A feeling I well knew, shame, and fear holding back the communication of what was really going on at home.

In those days without a job and with so much time alone, I began to paint prolifically. My first featured showing in a gallery was booked in Kennewick, and I needed to have 40 to 50 paintings for the showing. Keisha Cole and a glass of wine were my nightly accompaniments as I worked through pumping out those paintings. Singing, full of joy, those were the beautiful moments. Nighttime would inevitably bring the breakdowns.

Delivering the graduating speech for our class, I had been complimented by the Dean saying that it was the best student speech he had ever heard delivered. I had worked hard to graduate at the top of my class.

The notion that my grades and dedication would garner me a job soon was wiped away. I was still a stranger in this town. The girls who barely passed were given jobs. Girls who had friends in offices were promised jobs before they even graduated. I took the Certification test and finished a 3-hour test in 45 minutes, a record time for the school, and in doing it passed with a 97%, also one of the highest scores to come out of the school.

One of my classmates was given a job in a clinic I had applied to because she was friends with the administrator. She failed her certification test and would be forced to wait and retake it again later. It was then that I realized all my grades and work meant nothing, only the presence of the degree and who I knew or did not know.

The feeling of never being enough, of never being seen deepened, and despair dug deeper into my soul. What could I do? How would I ever be seen? Would anyone ever think I was enough? It weighed on me like a landslide of jagged shale pinning me down and holding me there unable to breath.

Running out of money and benefits, I was forced to begin selling off my possessions to pay the bills as I searched in vain for work. Finally, my best friend who had moved to Portland offered to let me stay with her and her fiancé while I searched for work there.

***

"No matter what kind of challenges or difficulties or painful situations you go through in your life, we all have something deep within us that we can reach down and find the inner strength to get through them."
Alana Stewart

***

Packing up what was left, I said goodbye to my daughter and grandson. As soon as I hit the freeway, tears flooded my eyes and pain filled my gut. I could not bear leaving my grandson, but I had no choice.

In the meantime, I had found a new gym—an old school, down and gritty iron gym. World competition for raw or classic lifters had not yet begun. If I wanted to compete at that level, I would have to learn to use those suits that assisted equipment. My good friend, coach, and multi-time world champion in Hawaii sent me a suit, and I began the process of learning to use one.

People think it's so simple as just putting on a suit and magically your numbers go up 100 plus pounds. Not so! Those things are tight, impossible to put on, and they have a "groove" that can toss you around if you're not lifting properly. That plus the extreme choking pain of a tight knee wrap, makes it hard to even focus on the lift, at least the first several times.

A quick cycle training in the equipment, and I competed in a qualifying meet up in Washington to allow me to head to Nationals in the spring. Returning to Oregon, I began training for Nationals a second time. January, working on my squat, I had been having issues since returning from the hip replacement surgery. I leaned instead of "sitting" causing the bar to jut forward on my shoulders and forcing me into a failing position.

Training at Kabuki in Portland, the suit was put on, I stepped into a piece of equipment called a Monolift to set up for my lift. The monolift utilizes webbing straps for safeties, instead of bars like seen in most squat racks. Stepping up to the bar loaded with 300 pounds, I assessed the placement of the straps and proceeded to push them out to the side further. The coach working with me decisively pushed them back inward toward my hands. I cautioned that the position would catch my hands if I failed. The response was to "shut up and lift".

The weight was not too much. I was just getting used to the suit and sitting into it finding the groove and achieving the proper depth. Down I sank into the squat position, coming up I leaned, and the suit shoved me forward. I could not finish the lift. The spotter was not paying attention. I quickly looked to see how far the straps were from the bar and made the split-second decision to dump it into the straps rather than risk injuring my back from the poor position.

I felt the bar hit the straps as I hit my knees under the bar. Pain shot through my right hand. I pulled, it would not move. Again, I pulled. It went nowhere. Now that I had the attention of the spotters, I yelled for them to lift the bar off me. It took some further yelling to get them to understand I could not move because my thumb was under the bar.

As I felt the bar come off my hand, I pulled it and immediately flipped it palm up knowing my thumb was gone. I could not bring myself to look at it. The spotter saw it and stumbled to the edge of the platform heaving as if to throw up.

A towel was quickly wrapped around my hand, I was given some ibuprophen, and off to the ER I went. Thank God, I was wearing wrist wraps. They acted as a tourniquet and kept the thumb from bleeding until we were almost to the ER.

Rushing inside, I laid my thumb on the counter and began to tell them what had happened. I was so calm (shock had taken over). The receptionist insisted on unwrapping my thumb to take a look. I strongly cautioned that it would not be a good idea. I even told her in no uncertain terms that she needed to put something down to catch the blood before uncovering it or face the task of contamination remediation. She did not listen. My thumb was unwrapped, and blood went flowing everywhere—over the countertop, down over the papers in front of her, and all onto the floor.

At most 30 seconds passed before a wheelchair came and scooped me up taking me to a room. One by one, four different doctors came in to look. Four different doctors refused to attempt replacing it.

Sitting on the gurney, bored, and still in shock, I took pictures of that thumb and posted them on FB. I'm surprised they were not taken down! It was gruesome.

A doctor from Emmanuel hospital across town agreed to take a look. Packed up and placed in an ambulance, I took the ride to the new hospital. Pain meds kicking in, I no longer cared.

The doctor finally came in and took a look and said, "See you in the morning." What? He was not going to work on it tonight? Why?

LIFTED UP

I have a thumb today thanks to that doctor. I was later told that he waited overnight to see if I still had color in the thumb in the morning. Color meant there was enough blood supply left to save the thumb. Grey would mean he would be amputating instead.

***

"Strength does not come from winning. Your struggles develop your strengths. When you go through hardships and decide not to surrender, that is strength."
Arnold Schwarzenegger

***

I was restricted from lifting. I had to have two sources of blood supply and that is all I had left. Lifting and increased blood flow could compromise that and cost me my thumb. I couldn't lift for 6 weeks, and then it was to be only very light lifting.

Of course, this meant I would not be going to Nationals that year. Crud. I would try again the following year!

Friends should never move in with friends, especially when there is a new relationship involved. I heard far too much from her about his neglect, his narcissism, his complete selfishness, and suspected indiscretions. Conflict ensued, and I was soon looking for a new place to live. Thumb still only 2 weeks out from surgery, I found myself searching for a home.

Thank goodness, I had found a job. My first days at the new job started with what I called my Franken thumb. Pins sticking out, stitches wrapping around it, and all neatly encased in a custom black sheath.

It was tough waiting those few months to begin lifting again, but I wanted to keep my thumb. Slowly, I worked my way back into lifting. I decided to stick to raw lifting, because there was now a World Championship for raw lifters.

My strength came back quickly. By Fall, I had qualified for Nationals yet again. One more time, training began in preparation for national competition.

This time, I had unwittingly gotten myself involved with a man who had a sketchy past. The cost of legalities to try and keep him from contacting me drained my resources, and I could not afford to go.

My phone rang. It was my son. The voice on the other end was stern and matter of fact, "Mom, I want you to move, closer to either me or Minda. I don't like you being in the city all alone where we can't get to you."

I told him I would think about it. I had built a life in Portland. I had my own medical clinic to work and was no longer traveling as a floater. I had built a rapport with some local lifters and was just appointed State Chair for the Oregon Chapter of USA Powerlifting. I loved Portland, loved the rain, loved the diversity, and loved the energy.

A couple of days passed, and I called him back. I would move to Boise to be near him. It was a decision I was uneasy with, as I knew it would mean an end to my social life. I was worried about finding an adequate gym. I was not looking forward to the quiet Idaho life and attitude again.

I did, however, look forward to being near my son again and being near family.

The search for work began. Several trips were made to interviews, and I found a job. Each trip, I toted a few of my belongings along with me. One last trip and the remainder of my things arrived in Boise.

LIFTED UP

CHAPTER 25

THE REALIZATION

"She was powerful, not because she wasn't scared but because she went on so strongly despite the fear."
Atticus

Powerlifting had become my life. It was everything that was important to me. Way back in the beginning, my son had teased me, stating that I was stronger than other women. We teased back and forth until he blurted out a challenge. He said if I was going to spend so much time and effort and potentially money on this sport, I had better do something with it. He expected me to become a world champion. I accepted the challenge. Then he turned the tables on me, he looked me in the eye and made me promise him. I could not back down now. I looked him dead in the eye and promised.

I may not have been a perfect parent, I certainly made my share of horrid mistakes, but there was one thing I strove to do right—if I promised the kids, I moved hell and high water to make sure it happened. There were plenty of "Oh yeah, I'll take care of that" things that got forgotten or not completed, but I tried to instill in them a faith in me that said, "If Mom pinky swears (promises), I know it will get done." I had not broken a solemn promise since that commitment had been made in the early days after the divorce.

Now what? What on earth had I done? As the brevity of that promise began to sink in and the depth of tasks I would need to achieve to make it happen, I wondered how I would make it happen.

LIFTED UP

To achieve that promise would mean I would have to compete at a local level and achieve a total (the sum of the best of the 3 lifts, squat, bench and deadlift) that would allow me to move forward to Nationals. Once at Nationals, I would have to win my age and weight class to get invited to represent the US the following year at World Championships. Once there, I would have to win one more time. There are over 90 countries associated with our parent federation, and any number of them may bring competitors to that event.

Training began again once in Boise. I had worked hard to fix the flaws in my squat and increase my deadlift. Bench, on the other hand, had been giving me issues.

Once again, I qualified for National competition. Once again, training began in preparation. This would be the 4th year I had qualified. I was laser focused, pushing myself harder than ever. I had to win. Losing was not an option.

February, everything was right on track. Doing a movement to strengthen my posterior chain, I felt a slight strain. Two days later, my left knee was swollen so badly that it measured 8 inches bigger around than the right knee. I could hardly walk.

NO! Not again. This could not be happening again.

The knee never healed. The swelling continued. Training was excruciating. Every cell in my body screamed that I should give up. Friends and co-workers resoundingly seconded that.

My heart sank. Why? Why did this keep happening? What was wrong? I had to be more! I could not let Mom be right. I had to make Pappa proud.

Over the past several years, I had begun to piece together all the tools that had been delivered to me in life and to try and heal that entire old trauma. I had started working with my subconscious to break up that old patterning and allow a different future for myself. I no longer spend nights crying begging to be taken.

"Permanence, perseverance and persistence in spite of all obstacles, discouragements, and impossibilities:
It is this, that in all things distinguishes the strong soul from the weak."
Thomas Carlyle

Looking back at the things that had happened, I recognized the constant pattern of getting so far and then having something happen to stop the progress—a subconscious block, a glass ceiling, a self-imposed limitation. All those years of being told I would never amount to anything and being told I would never achieve anything great. A lifetime of messages dumped on me of how I was not and would never be enough. Those were not going to be my story any longer. Those were someone else's story.

This promise to my son was now a promise to myself. A promise to overcome, to break free from all that negativity, and to be somebody. I felt the deep need to do something just for me, to follow through, and not give up. I wanted my life to have meaning and to have a better story. I wanted my Pappa in heaven to smile down with pride that his girl never gave up.

LIFTED UP

The mind is a powerful thing. The realization of the depth of my dysfunction began to settle in. My subconscious had been so strongly engrained with those messages that I took on in that heavy cloak of invisibility and "not enough". My subconscious believed it so strongly that every time I neared a point of breaking past the limitations I had so long accepted, it made sure I sat down and stayed in my place. Even if my conscious mind did not understand my place, my subconscious had been there to take the reins and make sure I did not exceed those limitations.

Manifesting in physical damage, financial loss, and emotional despair, my subconscious had been doing its job.

Of course, I cried, but then I got mad! Then I found hope and determination. I began in earnest putting to use all the tools at my disposal to reprogram my subconscious.

"You have power over your mind - not outside events. Realize this, and you will find strength."

Marcus   Aurelius

Focused completely on breaking this pattern now took the lead, and the competitions took second place in importance. Whatever it took, I was going to go to Nationals. Even if I could only squat the bar, I was going, and I was going to stand on that platform. I would change my story one small step at a time.

Limping, barely able to walk most days, people thought I was insane. Others could not wrap their head around why this meant so much to me. Solid determination pushed me forward. Tired of feeling inadequate and playing small. I was going to go and change my story.

One month out, the knee still hurt bad enough that I was on crutches. Voices came in from all sides telling me to stop, "You can't even walk. How are you going to compete?"

I shut all those voices out and focused on breaking a lifetime of patterns that caused me pain.

The time came. I finally made it to Nationals. It was the biggest powerlifting competition in the Nation to date, the largest regardless of federation or affiliation. Over a thousand lifters were there. Icons. Lifters who I had watched for years were there. I felt blessed to be amongst them all.

"Out of suffering have emerged the strongest souls; the most massive characters are seared with scars. "
Khalil Gibran

My roommate and teammate watched me limping heavily the day before I was to lift. "Misha, you can't lift tomorrow. You can barely walk!" My message was loud and clear. I would give my best, but at the very least I was taking the platform.

Heart racing, nerves tingling, I could barely feel my knee. My name was called, and I took the platform for my opening squat. Nerves kicked in, my head swimming; I looked down at my feet, something I never do in practice. I bobbled, felt the weight on my back sway, and I almost fell over. Pulling myself together, I stood solid and waited for my commands. White lights! The squat was good, and I was now officially on my way to having competed at Nationals.

As it turned out, none of my competitors came that year. Their last-minute decisions not to come left me as the sole competitor in my age and weight class. It did not matter. I was going to compete as if they were there. I knew the numbers they were capable of and my goal was to put up numbers that would win me the competition even if they had shown up. Mission accomplished. I finished the meet, set new American records in all three lifts, and earned my bid for the slot on the National team.

Had I listened to my small inner voice and to all those who encouraged me to give up, I would have never stood there that day. I would never have gotten the email that said I was invited to the National team!

One step down, but the World Championship had not yet been won. I had to stay focused, continue the work, and continue to break past my own barriers.

I took a second job to afford the trip. Worlds would be in Finland. Nothing was going to stop me! There were moments when finances were tight, and I was not sure I would make it.

In fact, my car was totaled in an early morning accident a few months out. This accident required money for a new car and deductibles. Still I refused to give up on me. I was on a roll. No matter what came my way, I would overcome it.

Settling the finances, my right shoulder was torn by repeated use holding onto a morbidly obese client who fought as we tried to give her care. My arm dislocated every week. I could not use it to pull up my pants, drive, or clean myself after the restroom. Just another challenge to make sure I was serious about breaking this barrier. As if the universe was saying, "Are you really serious this time?"

"Where there is no struggle, there is no strength."
Oprah Winfrey

MISHA FAYANT

It was painful trying to hold the bar against my shoulders. As I squatted, it brought tears to my eyes. I stayed focused knowing that what was really at stake was my life! I studied my competition, studied those who had come before me, and I prepared.

Sitting on the plane, the long flight over the pond towards Finland, I held back tears. Listening to a self-hypnosis track I made for this event over and over, I stayed focused during the flight.

Standing on the platform, holding the little American Flag I was handed, it did not hit me until our National Anthem was played. I did it! I triumphed! I was now a World Champion. In the process, I set new world records in bench press and squat. I swore I would not cry. The salty taste hit my lips as the tears rolled off my cheeks. These were tears of joy, of relief; of knowing I had achieved something great against all odds. I bucked the system, gave my subconscious the finger, and chose to re-write my story.

Through all the pain, through all the challenges, I finally stopped giving up on me, and finally had realized that no one would save me but ME! I felt so empowered, so new, and full of hope. This would be my story now. No more hiding, and no more playing small. No more allowing someone else's crap to cloud my view.

This book is for you, the reader. I want you to know no matter what, you are enough. You can change your story. You can achieve greatness and move past the pain.

YOU must make the choice to move forward. I invite you to take that step and find your own superhero story within your life. Stand in your greatness and shine!

LIFTED UP

""Can you see the rainbow emerge from your storm?
It's there. You will find it when you look for it."
Misha Fayant

MISHA FAYANT

I'M STILL STANDING

"You could never know what it's like
Your blood like winter freezes just like ice
And there's a cold lonely light that shines from you
You'll wind up like the wreck you hide behind that mask you use

And did you think this fool could never win
Well look at me, I'm coming back again
I got a taste of love in a simple way
And if you need to know
while I'm still standing you just fade away

Don't you know I'm still standing better than I ever did
Looking like a true survivor, feeling like a little kid
I'm still standing after all this time
Picking up the pieces of my life without you on my mind"

Elton John

ACKNOWLEDGEMENTS

There are so many who have contributed to my journey. My father, rest his soul, gave me purpose, vision, and resilience. He was my rock.

My children Minda Waits, (my angel and gentle support) Damon Waits (My protagonist and antagonist, master of accountability).

My coaches Gene Bell and Anthony Harris, the lifters along the way who supported me as I grew, Kevin Stewart, Ken Gack, Colleen Hansford, Mary Ellen Stansbury-Hodges, Joaquin Diaz-Deleon, Sam Mitchell, Bonica Brown, and so many others.

The childhood friends who always had my back Teresa Cartwright, Tamra Hiatt, Dannis Nyberg.

The many spiritual teachers who held my soul as I healed, learned and grew. Carmen Murray, Lavonda, Laurinda Nosiglia (to name only a few).

Every single person who has been a part of my life has contributed to my story and I thank you all for your participation in it.

MISHA FAYANT

May 16, 2018

Unexpected tears today. I did so much meditating and praying last night—thinking about Pappa, my heritage, and what it all means. To stand on the podium and represent the US as a Native American/First Nations Woman is the proudest and most humbling thing for me. The Eagle represents Pappa, that's why I'm holding this Native American flag.

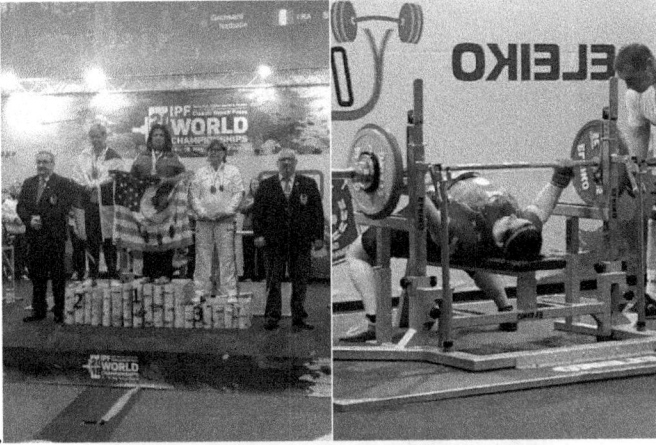

LIFTED UP

SPEAKER / AUTHOR/ BREAKTHROUGH COACH / HEALER

Misha Fayant

**KEYNOTE SPEAKER/
SEMINARS/
BREAKTHROUGH SESSIONS**

- OVERCOMING
- GOAL SETTING
- "I AM ENOUGH,
  YOU ARE ENOUGH"
- "STRONG FROM THE
  INSIDE OUT"
- REPROGRAMMING THE
  PAST FOR A BETTER
  FUTURE
- SELF ACCOUNTABILITY
  FOR SUCCESS

CONNECT WITH ME

f   mishafayant

⌾   mishafayant

▶   mishafayant

in   MishaFayant5230054

WHAT OTHERS SAY ABOUT HER

"Without you my future would have been different
than what it is now . . ."

"an accomplished inspiration for all women and girls
of all ages . . ."

"I was at a standstill in my spiritual journey until we
finally came together . . ."

WWW.MISHAFAYANT.COM
WWW.MPOWEREDLIVES.COM
Email: info@mishafayant.com

Mpowered
Lives